W9-AGN-176

The Writer's Workshop

Imitating Your Way to Better Writing

Gregory L. Roper

ISI
BOOKS

Wilmington, Delaware

Copyright © 2007 ISI Books
Second paperback printing, 2012

All rights reserved. No part of this publication may be reproduced or transmitted in any form or by any means, electronic or mechanical, including photocopy, or any information storage and retrieval system now known or to be invented, without permission in writing from the publisher, except by a reviewer who wishes to quote brief passages in connection with a review written for inclusion in a magazine, newspaper, or broadcast.

Roper, Gregory L.

   The writer's workshop : imitating your way to better writing / Gregory L. Roper. — 1st ed. — Wilmington, Del. : ISI Books, 2007.

     p. ; cm.

     ISBN: 978-1-933859-33-0
     Includes bibliographical references.

     1. English language—Composition and exercises. 2. English language—Rhetoric—Study and teaching. 3. English language—Grammar—Study and teaching. I. Title.

PE1404 .R66 2007   2007933852
808/.0420711—dc22   0710

Passage from Cicero taken from *Selected Political Speeches*, translated and introduced by Michael Grant (Penguin Classics, 1969). Copyright © Michael Grant Publications Limited, 1969. Reproduced by permission of Penguin Books Ltd. Excerpt from *A Portrait of the Artist as a Young Man*, by James Joyce, copyright 1916 by B. W. Huebsch, copyright 1944 by Nora Joyce, copyright © 1944 by the Estate of James Joyce. Used by permission of Viking Penguin, a division of Penguin Group (USA) Inc. Excerpt from G. K. Chesterton, *The Man Who Was Thursday*, used by permission of A P Watt Ltd. on behalf of The Royal Literary Fund. Passage from Brian Tierney, *The Crisis of Church and State, 1030–1300,* reprinted with the permission of Simon & Schuster Adult Publishing Group. Copyright © 1964 by Prentice-Hall Inc.; copyright renewed © 1992 by Brian Tierney. Passage from *The Short Stories of Ernest Hemingway* reprinted with permission of Scribner, an imprint of Simon & Schuster Adult Publishing Group. Copyright 1933 by Charles Scribner's Sons. Copyright renewed © 1961 by Mary Hemingway. Passage from Thomas Aquinas's *Summa Theologica* used by permission of Ave Maria Press, all rights reserved.

book design by Beer Editorial and Design
manufactured in the United States of America

ISI Books
Intercollegiate Studies Institute
3901 Centerville Road
Wilmington, Delaware 19807-1938
www.isibooks.org

Contents

Preface

Most composition textbooks these days, though well-meaning, are dreary, predictable affairs, although for years I used many of them in attempts to help my *Introduction to Composition 101* (or equivalent) students improve their writing. Most try to introduce students to basic modes of writing (narrative, explanatory, persuasive, etc.). And most give examples from the standard sources of essay writing today, especially the general-interest political-cultural organs like the *New Yorker,* the *Atlantic, Harper's,* and so on. Somewhat regularly, students reading these texts also get to read student essays that try to mimic the styles of these magazines. This leads to a monotone treatment of writing both in content and in style. The content that the composition texts invariably feature is from a political viewpoint steadily left of center. The occasional op-ed piece from the *Wall Street Journal* is just as inevitably included as a straw man, or a sop to the notion of presenting fairly both sides of an issue, though it is abundantly clear which side the editors of the textbook favor. But in some ways worse, for pedagogical reasons, is the monotone in style: all of the texts feature that contemporary conversational essay style so favored by such periodicals, a style that hides its very structure, that displays a voice not too distinctive as to offend.

I came to believe, through years of teaching, that it is the very sameness of the examples, especially in form though also in content, that was making it difficult for me to teach my students to write well. I could, using the better of these texts, get the students to learn something about description, about building a decent narrative, even—with hard work and revision—building a reasonably competent argument. But there was so little *life* to the writing, so seldom a living *voice* coming from these students, who were, I knew, full of fascination—with interesting pasts, complex family lives, sometimes startling viewpoints—and burning with things to tell the world. And structure, at both the paragraph and sentence levels, was extremely difficult for students to learn; it seemed that either they had it or they did not.

At the same time, I was turning from my composition classes to my literature classes, where I was talking every day about structure and style, voice, metaphor and analogy. I was talking about the inevitable connection between form and content, why *how* the writer said something was impossible to divide from *what* he was saying. I was talking about how Chaucer adapted his sources to produce something entirely new, how Shakespeare was learning from Ovid yet arguing with him, and suggesting to the students that it was precisely in this creative rethinking of the tradition, of talking back to their influences, that Chaucer, Shakespeare, Milton, and the Coen Brothers found what they had to say in their art. And I spoke to the literature students of where these writers learned this—in their earliest classrooms, where they were forced to imitate, often in very strict ways, the "greats" of their tradition. Rhetorical instruction, I told them, was based for over two thousand years on imitation, and our current separation of style and ornament (rarely if at all covered in the composition textbooks) from invention and arrangement would have seemed backwards and foolish for much of Western culture's history of teaching writing.

So I tore up my syllabi and began to teach students in a different way. First, I changed the content: no more tepid *New Yorker* prose; we would go to the greats, learn from the real masters whose prose had stood the test of time. And we would learn by imitating these masters, just as they learned. I wanted to highlight strange forms, structures, and especially voices: I wanted different ordering strategies to smack my students upside of their heads, so to speak, and to have them hear people who did not sound a bit like a friendly intelligent conversational moderately liberal coast-dweller. Strangely, it worked. They could see a clear structure in a fourteenth-century text they could not discover in a late-twentieth-century one; they could find a lively voice in a nineteenth-century novelist they could not find in a contemporary magazine writer. Relevance, one could say, is overrated. Students felt challenged, believed they were finally connecting with writers who could help them improve, and did improve, often in far greater leaps than they had in any previous writing course. This should not be a surprise, since it worked for two and a half millennia, yet it is a surprise to many in the rhet/comp business today.

I hope this book and the exercises it contains can help you, whether you are a teacher looking for new ways to help your students improve their writing, or a young writer looking to teach yourself; both can use this book with profit. I do think this book could be used quite profitably in a standard classroom, by homeschoolers, or by the autodidact looking to improve her own writing on her own time.

I might offer a few words of explanation of some of the book's oddities before you begin.

First, this is a book you must do, not just read, both as a teacher and as a student. The exercises are crucial; you must imitate your way to better writing, not just think about doing so by looking at the examples. Thus you must apply yourself to use this book well. Try the exercises. Don't cheat ahead to see "how it's done." This goes for teachers as well as students—colleagues, try the exercises yourselves, and see what you discover. And please read the "To the Teacher" and "To the Student" sections to help you get a start on "doing" the book.

Second, expect challenges. I will never say that this will be easy, only that it will be worth it. Struggle a bit, and accept that. Some readers of this book—from presses that rejected it—were sure it would be too difficult for their students. I do not agree, and I have the experience to prove it: I have taught this material to freshmen in a regional state university with relatively open admissions, to students at a very selective private school with a demanding core curriculum of the Great Books, and to many audiences in between. You will see student examples in each chapter showing that you can achieve this level of excellence. Do not fall for the lie that today's students cannot do what medieval or early modern or ancient students did every day of their lives, often at much younger ages. They did it, and so can today's students. I have seen it for myself on a daily basis.

Third, do not be afraid to step out after a while and try your own way. I do recommend that you, as teacher or student, try to stick to the assignments (and their sequence) for a good while, but you may find yourself wanting to shake up the sequence after a bit, or try new models for your imitations. Good. Now you have the point—that this process of learning by imitation is what all writers do, all the time, if they want to stay alive, to keep learning. What I offer here is a framework for setting up a workshop, not an overly prescriptive design for how to run it.

Fourth, reflect often upon what you are doing here, whether teacher or student. I do not intend the tasks to be mechanical exercises, but doorways into a richer world of language, metaphor, description, experience. I have included sections on Great Ideas precisely in order to encourage such larger thinking, and I have asked students to complete tasks so as to begin reflecting on their writing as functioning in a larger world of their discourse, their interaction with ideas, and with their souls. Leave time and room for this as you approach the book, and I suspect that you will find not just your writing improving, but your world expanding.

August 2007

Acknowledgments

*T*his book would not exist without my friend and former colleague Keith Rhodes. It was he who first thought I had something of an idea; it was he who encouraged me to pursue it. He lent his considerable knowledge of the rhetoric/composition world to the project, and worked producing a second half of the text for several years. When the first presses failed to see the book's virtues, Keith never wavered in thinking that we were on to something, and his judicious mind and thoughtful comments have made every page of this book better. When he chose to leave the project, it was with much regret on both sides, and it is with happiness that I thank him first of all for any success this book might have.

I want to thank the University of Dallas for the financial and administrative support that allowed me to complete the book, including a summer faculty grant that helped me take it from the Roper-Rhodes combination to the single-author text it is today. Each of my colleagues in the Department of English has encouraged and helped me, but I want to thank a few in particular. David Davies found the book fascinating from the first time I mentioned it in an MLA interview, and has provided critical help along the way. The twinkle in his eye when I told this classicist I asked my writing students to imitate Cicero, and his knowledge of Renaissance pedagogy, were equally valuable to me; he has read carefully and critically parts of the manuscript. Scott Crider showed immediate interest, and through his conversation, always thoughtful and generous critical comments, and support, he improved the book in many ways. He also directed me to John Briggs, whose helpful criticism I want to acknowledge. John Sommerfeldt read and improved enormously the two chapters on medieval subjects. Gerard Wegemer has been a calm and encouraging voice throughout my work here. Karen Gempel, the administrative assistant who knows all and does everything well, from Texas flora to the intricacies of Braniff Hall life, deserves my deep thanks as well, and I wish to render it on this page.

Jeremy Beer has been a steady and guiding hand at ISI Books, and it is of course due to his faith in the value of this method that you are reading this book today.

It was my parents who first gave me a love of the word; my father passed on his rich southern heritage of speech, and my mother was always the sharpest at pressing me to argue well, to choose words precisely and carefully (most memorably when she took a bleeding red pen to the high school newspaper of which I was then editor in chief), to express myself clearly. Their love of truth and dedication to character and integrity formed me in a warm world of love. No man could wish for better parents.

I want to thank my many students at Northwest Missouri State University and the University of Dallas who have been diligent and thoughtful in working through courses and assignments, in telling me what works and what does not work in the teaching of writing. Those whose work appears in this book deserve my thanks, but so do the many whose work, often equally impressive, does not. They have all made me a better teacher, and what more can one ask of one's students?

So to all of these, and many others who remain nameless, including a very fine copy editor at ISI Books, I offer my gratitude. If there are faults in the book, they remain mine, despite the best efforts of these and others.

The book is dedicated to my wife and sons, in thanks for all of their patience and help during all the days and nights I should have been spending in care of them but instead was grading, commenting, writing. They are my domestic church, my conduit to the divine, and without the love they allow me to bask in, I and my words are merely a sounding brass, a clanging cymbal.

To the Student:
On Becoming an "Apprentice"

Nature is commonplace.
Imitation is more interesting.

–Gertrude Stein

*I*ndulge me for a moment by using your historical imagination. You live in Florence in the fifteenth century; you come from that burgeoning middle class of merchants and artisans and are training to be a painter. Your father has apprenticed you to one of the well-known painters of the day, and for years now, since you were quite a youngster, you have worked your way up in his workshop. First you merely swept the floors, cleaned up the dyes and tints and frames and such at the end of the day; then you learned to mix the paints. After years you were allowed to do fill-in work on small compositions; gradually your master gave you parts of compositions to complete. More recently you've been learning the new art of single-point perspective; you've been learning your master's style; his way of arranging figures and shading and color; the sorts of compositions, religious and, more recently, secular images from the Greek myths, that the master uses. At the same time, you've been learning the business of being a painter: the delicate and yet competitive process of securing commissions from patrons, the troubles of securing materials, of securing apprentices like yourself, of paying assistants to help in the largest projects. You have confidence that, if your master were to ask you to produce a crucifix for a new church, you could make one so good that few, if any, would know the difference between your work and your master's. At the same time, you've begun to think that you might see things a bit differently, have your own styles you'd like to try—perhaps different subject matter, perhaps new ways of handling color and line and shading. Of course you don't do these in your work for the master, but you've begun experimenting a bit on your own. He's taught you well, and you feel ready to produce your Master Piece, that first piece of work that will show that you, too, can be a Master, open a workshop, obtain commissions, have apprentices and assistants of your own.

Or you are a jazz musician. You were first attracted to the music by its energy, style, artfulness, the freedom of improvising—of making it up as you went along, of the freedom to play whatever you wanted, rather than having to follow the notes on the page someone else had written. Of course that was years ago. Since then you've realized that to do that well, you have to know chords and scales and modulations and patterns—in fact, an enormous amount of musical theory—quite well, and you've memorized and practiced these over and over again. But not only that. As you met other jazz musicians, you found that you wanted to learn their phrasings, their "licks," their snippets. And they told you they had learned these from others. So like many jazz musicians, you went back to study the greats—Charlie "Bird" Parker, Dizzy Gillespie, Miles Davis—writing out their most famous solos and memorizing them until you could play them in your sleep. Of course you soon realized that no one wanted to hear you play a copy of a Diz solo, but doing this gave you a closetful of resources, phrases, licks, out of which you began to construct your own distinctive style.

❧

I give you these two vignettes because in them is bound up the central method of this book: imitation of the greats as a way to learn an art and develop into an accomplished artist oneself. It is, in fact, the way almost all crafts, all arts, have been learned throughout history, from blacksmithing to shoemaking to jazz to, yes, writing. Shakespeare, Chaucer, Milton, and countless others learned the art of writing in a school system that, in teaching Latin, forced these students to translate and imitate the great classical writers of antiquity, over and over again. It instilled in them a respect for these writers, for they knew intimately not just the things the writers said, but the rhythms and patterns of their prose, the meters and shadings of their poetry. Like the jazz musicians, Milton could imitate effects from Virgil (and Homer, and the Bible, and more) in *Paradise Lost* because from the time he was quite young he had read, translated, and imitated the *Aeneid* over and over. And he could make a new kind of English poetry by discovering his own voice in adopting and adapting these masters.

Now, few writing books on the market today teach you to write by making this method the important step in learning. Some of them suggest that if you just express your inner self enough, through free-writing and such, you'll figure out how to write well just by constantly saying what's inside of you. Others explore writing as politics (usually from the left), and encourage you to see writing as a negotiation between your situation and the power structures around you. Still others tell you about the basic forms—of assembling an essay (intros, bodies, conclusions), of argument (definitional, causal, evaluative, etc.)—and have you try your hand at assembling the writing through working on mastering these forms. All of them have a grasp on a piece of the truth, but all of them, as G. K. Chesterton says of heretics, think their piece of the truth is the whole truth. Writing is at times self-expression, but not always, and self-expression alone is not going to teach you the crafts and skills necessary to organize and assemble a complex piece of prose. (Imagine setting a young painting student in front of a canvas and saying, "Just paint what you feel," and telling him little else: how would he learn the techniques of perspective, shading, line, composition? And how many of us have heard awful solos, in jazz or rock, from musicians who just "play what they feel" without any knowledge of the craft of good music?) And indeed, writing is political—as is painting, as is jazz—but it is also much more, and focusing on political engagement is not going to teach us how to craft sentences better, or organize our thoughts better so others can understand them and be persuaded by them. And yes, it is important to know something about basic forms in writing, but just being told about them does not help much; like the jazz musician, you have to know the forms intimately, and you do so by following the contours of those forms the great ones constructed.

So what should you do if you want to learn how to write? (And I suppose you do, if you are holding this book right now.) Well, this book suggests that you learn writing the way it (and all other arts) have been taught, at least in Western culture, and in fact in many others as well, for over 2,500 years—by imitating the greats, the accomplished writers from the past who are almost universally acknowledged as masters. That is, to learn to write better,° you must become an apprentice, working under a series of masters in a Writer's Workshop.

What I have arranged here, then, is a brief beginning of that process. In using this book, you often will have a text from a great writer set before you, and you will attempt to imitate his or her writing. You will be like the Florentine painter, learning how to mimic every move of your master. And I encourage you to do this—try to imitate small things, like syntax, or metaphors; try to get at the rhythm of the writer's sentences; try to grasp the larger movements that make up the writer's sensibility, his worldview, if you will. Become an apprentice, and enjoy the fact that you are apprenticing with some of the real masters of us-

---

* You already write pretty well. I'm quite sure of that, too, if you are holding this book right now. If you do not believe me, take a look at some recent essay you have written. Now imagine you are just learning the English language for the first time—can you see all of the complex rules, requirements, and idioms you are using, and using well, without even realizing it? If you do not, try translating the essay into some language you are taking or have recently taken in a class—Spanish, French, Russian, whatever. Or try writing an original essay in that language. You'll quickly see how much more fluent you are writing in English. So the point is not to write well for the first time, but to write better. And I know you need to do that, not just because you are holding this book, but because we all need to do that, all the time. And we need to do that because better writing enlarges our minds, gives us a greater mental universe in which to exist, opens and leads our souls in different and new ways.

ing words. I will lead you through a series of masters, each with something to teach you, something to enlarge your competence and ability and world.

Realize, too, that imitation is not just a matter of learning technical skills. Imitation can lead to deeper, further knowledge. A few years ago, my friend Keith Rhodes took up the electric bass. He thought that the way to do it would be to learn from one of the masters. So he got out all his old Beatles albums—I know, they are well before your time, and in fact a little before mine, but indulge me here for a minute—and started playing along with Paul McCartney's bass work, from *Help* to *Let It Be*. He learned so many of the "moves," the riffs, the "tricks," but he also, he told me, thinks he discovered something about the Beatles. The standard rock-critic opinion is that John Lennon was the real artist of the group, McCartney just a pop-song writer. But seeing the songs from McCartney's viewpoint, because he was imitating him, Keith had an intimate knowledge of McCartney's work in the group. He began to see how McCartney grew more as an artist than any other Beatle. Maybe the group broke up—that *awful* event for the '60s generation!—because he just wanted to find musicians who would grow along with him, and he felt John, George, and Ringo were not going to grow musically. McCartney's playing, his inventive writing, came forth to my friend in a new way, and Keith says he would never have seen this had he not played along with him—imitated him, learned from him—in a careful, systematic way.

Imitation is not going to trap you into doing what everyone else has always done. On the contrary, it frees you to find your own individual way of doing things, by giving you the grounding for writing as the champions have always done. As I said, musicians almost all learn by the method I have described—patterning themselves on the great ones, then branching out on their own. Writers do the same. If you don't believe me, look at any short list of writers who were schooled in imitation and have developed some of the most distinctive works in all of literature: William Shakespeare, John Milton, Jane Austen, T. S. (and George) Eliot.

One more thing. I always remember learning best when I was having fun. Sometimes this can be a hard thing to pull off in an academic setting. It is not even necessary that you have fun with this book in order to learn from it. Yet it really ought to be possible to have fun learning with this book, or at least more possible than usual. The activities and exercises often encourage you to take your imitation work in particular with a light heart. I have recently been watching *The Magic Schoolbus* with my two sons, and the unusual teacher on that show, Ms. Frizzle, is fond of saying, "Take chances! Get messy! Make mistakes!" This book will work best when you have that attitude of risk-taking, of trying something new in an imitation, of not worrying too much about making mistakes because you are taking chances and trying new moves. Many of my students have done their best work when they took this advice to heart, and it certainly makes the work go down more easily.

To the Teacher:
How This Book Really Works

> *To admire on principle, is the only way to imitate*
> *without loss of originality.*
> —Samuel Taylor Coleridge

Sometimes the germ of an idea can give one the best glimpse of its nature. The idea for this book came when my colleague Keith Rhodes stood in my office doorway at Northwest Missouri State University, where we both taught heavy course loads of composition to students strong and weak, eager and indifferent, talented and remedial. I voiced the cynical statement that even the incorrigibly optimistic comp teacher can state when he is tired: "I can tell in the first week which students have a chance to go on and do well."

"Yeah, I know," Keith said to me. "It's the ones who had a home life that includes reading—any kind of reading—the newspaper, *Newsweek*, anything. The others struggle, no doubt about it."

"Ah, but why?" I wondered. "Figure that out and we'll be able to help those strugglers."

Now we were thinking, considering, and because of that, optimistic teachers again. What do the readers have that the others do not? We decided it was a stock of sentences, paragraphs, whole pieces, that the readers heard in their heads that the non-readers never had. This is why straight grammar instruction often fails, Keith said to me: the readers don't need it, because they hear the good sentences and mimic them, and the non-readers never get good sentences in their heads through mere grammar study. Because both of us are interested in music and sports, we were off into analogies: jazz musicians who have a store of "riffs" or "licks" around which to construct an improvised solo; the store of movements of chord structures a composer can use, vary, or reject in putting together a sonata; athletes who practice daily trying out the "moves" of Maradona, Michael, or Magic. So what was the analogy to writing? It was not just sentence-combining, though that got at part of it. Writers do not just imitate sentences, they imitate *everything*, from their individual word choices—I remember when "annihilate" infected my writing at age 17—to sentence patterns to paragraph structures to large-scale generic devices. We thought of friends who had been the best young writers we knew: one could tell what they had been reading because their letters suddenly started sounding like Faulkner or Austen or even Beckett. They went on to have their own voices, but at some crucial stage after first fluency and before a fully developed prose, they imitated their way to good writing, strong writing, writing with a supple, complex, alive voice. In other words, they had read carefully and deeply, apprenticing themselves to the marvelous writers they were encountering.

Could I teach that? As a teacher, I was not satisfied with it happening ad hoc, willy-nilly. I wondered if I could create structures so that this apprenticeship would happen more often in the classrooms I was responsible for leading. The result is the book you now hold.

Imitation and Apprenticeship

Thanks to research and thinking in the composition field, we now know some things that do not work terribly well in writing classes, and some things that do. We know that much of the learning about writing happens indirectly. We know that, as

Richard Haswell says, students value our classes even when they forget—or reject—much of the specifics of what we have taught them. We know that grammar lessons *alone* do not improve writing much, if at all. A pedagogy of exhortation accomplishes little; simply telling students to write in certain ways, or to compose their introductions to include certain features, does little good. Students regularly prove that they lose most of what they gain from direct and formulaic approaches, whether featuring processes or products, as quickly as they forget the factual details they learn in other courses. We do know that long and deep reading is the only sure way to improve writing, and that the students must *write*—that is, they must do it, rather than talk about it or be told about it. So we teachers need to give them methods for opening up their eyes and loosening up their hands, then preparing them to envision and apprehend new ways of writing when they encounter them.

What I create in this textbook, then, is a structured series of chapters, each of which has a carefully sequenced set of assignments, that lead the students to *think and read more carefully* about the writing we teachers set before them, and then, by *imitating* that writing, to consider it in even more detail, and produce far more complex writing than they had ever before been able to accomplish. I simply believe that the only method for learning writing is learning by doing, the same way one learns to play a violin, or hit a topspin forehand, or make a fine soufflé. Therefore, I ask students to become apprentice writers, standing beside an accomplished master just as an apprentice blacksmith or carpenter or electrician stands beside a professional, so the students learn the craft by watching, imitating, and then doing themselves. One step at a time. The students learn complex syntactical forms not in the abstract, but from seeing how Dickens, Cicero, or Paul of Tarsus uses them—or how James Joyce twists them. The students learn how to handle a counterargument by paying close attention to the balanced scholastic proofs of Aquinas, or that old foxy lawyer Cicero, and then trying it themselves.

This pedagogical insight is not new. It reaches back at least 2,500 years. Aristotle, who defined man as a rational animal and as a political animal elsewhere, in the *Poetics* defines man as an *imitative* animal, noting that children learn primarily by imitation and that we take delight in making imitations and in watching them (as on the stage). Virtually every writer one can think of in the West until at least the twentieth century was schooled in imitation as the primary method of learning to write—and every great writer in the twentieth century has confessed to learning this way, whether taught in school or not. Shakespeare, Milton, Chaucer, Lincoln: all had "the greats" set before them and were instructed from an early age to imitate their moves from the smallest stylistic devices (*occupatio, asyndeton*) to their larger organizational patterns. T. S. Eliot's "Tradition and the Individual Talent" is to a great extent a meditation on the power of this very process for producing great art. Jazz artists even today lovingly copy out every note of the great solos of Bird, Dizzy, and Satchmo in order to learn how they work. And today in Creative Writing classes *imitatio* is in many ways the fundamental method of instruction.

I am not just talking about stylistic tics here, but a deep form of learning. A jazz musician ultimately learns, if he studies them deeply enough, not just some Charlie Parker riffs and solos, but, the musicians themselves tell us, Parker's understanding of jazz, music theory, his voice, his understanding of life—and in so doing, the student begins to find his own voice, understanding, life. Most creative writing teachers say it is a pedagogical cliché that the instructor must get the Poetry Writing 101 students focusing on form (meter, stanzaic structure, etc.) so that they forget the "deep thoughts" the students so desperately want to convey in their poems and stories, and once that happens, more significant thoughts—and thus more accomplished narratives and lyrics—begin to emerge. *Imitatio* teaches then not just the final canon of rhetoric, ornamentation, but much more: it leads from invention, through arrangement, and beyond—as well as, I will admit, showing the student new methods of ornamentation. But literary scholars and rhetoricians have known for a long time—at least since Aristotle—that ornamentation is inseparable from argument, form from content. Thus, by focusing deeply on imitation, I ask students to enter—as it were, through the back door—to more significant writing.

And the goal here is not simply to have students who can write like Cicero, or produce a proof like Aquinas. Let us be honest: there are (perhaps sadly?) few public outlets for scholastic proofs these days, and only a few audiences (perhaps even more sadly?) want to read or hear Ciceronian prose outside of the classics department. But by apprenticing oneself to a master, one eventually begins to discover one's own voice, and in talking back to these masters, one develops one's own point of view. In their schooling, Chaucer, Shakespeare, Jonson, and Milton all were asked to imitate Ovid—often, repeatedly, carefully. Yet one could hardly find four more distinct voices in English literature, or four more different takes on Ovidianism. Similarly, Derek Walcott's great postmodern epic *Omeros*, which more than any work earned him the Nobel Prize, is inconceivable, and virtually opaque to the reader, without his deep knowledge of Homer, Virgil, Dante, Milton, Melville, and others, yet there is no mistaking that this is Walcott's West Indian voice speaking to us throughout, or that he is not merely rehashing old themes: his is an epic speaking about contemporary humans, in a contemporary voice, to contemporary readers.

How to Use This Book

I hope you will use this book by having your students *do* it, writing their way through the book. The chapters are not set up to have students read and learn a great deal of information; I do not substitute my own pedagogy of exhortation for the classroom's. Instead, each chapter is a carefully sequenced set of assignments that lead the students from their own free writing, through careful reading and analysis of a "master," to imitating that master, to reflecting on what they have learned through this process. In some chapters there is a sequence of sequences, with multiple masters, so that the students see how doing the same assignment under different masters produces vastly different writing, perceptions, knowledge. For instance, in chapter 2 students describe a set of events in their own voices, then attempt to describe the same set of events as Hemingway would describe them, then as James Joyce would. As you can see from this example, merely reading the two masters would be of little benefit; students must actually watch the diction, syntax, organization, and point of view change as they translate their own descriptions from Hemingway to Joyce, to learn that Hemingway and Joyce have not merely different stylistic tics, but inhabit vastly different mental universes. So again, *imitatio* is not merely a parlor trick, but it is the entry into all of the canons of rhetoric, from invention to ornament, showing students through their doing that form *is* content, content form.

I have broken the book into two sections.

Part 1, Foundations, lays the groundwork for crucial skills in any writing. In this section, students learn the crucial skill of describing the world around them, then investigating their worlds through defining terms and concepts. They learn from some of the great masters of description, definition, and exploration the many different ways these tasks may be accomplished, the many different skills the apprentice writer will want to master so as to render his world in words.

Part 2, Precision Tools and Finer Crafts, continues the carpentry metaphor and leads the students through a kind of modified mini-trivium, where students learn first the art of setting rules in place, and making the distinctions necessary, as well as creating a voice of proper authority that will convey the rules. Next, students learn the voice of careful logical distinction, and entertaining of counterarguments, from imitating Thomas Aquinas. I have found many times that the scholastic method embodied in Aquinas' prose of foregrounding the opposing side's arguments makes students into much more rhetorically aware essay writers. Finally, the students are led to complex persuasive writing through imitating Cicero's *Pro Archia*. I end by asking the students to imitate a delicate medieval interchange between pope and emperor so as to learn how building others' voices into one's own enables one to negotiate complex verbal, social, political, and cultural situations.

At two points in the book, I have included a section called "Reflection." In these I ask the students to begin to reflect on what they have learned, how their writing is improving, and what they might like to accomplish next. You will by now have seen the pattern: the students begin with the self, lose the self in the imitation of the master, and return to the self in the Reflections.

Working through the book therefore becomes a dialectic between apprenticing oneself to older masters—in order to experience a sense of disjunction, in order to master a set of skills by working in a voice that sounds quite "other"—and coming back to the self to see how that experience has broadened and deepened the experiences, thoughts, and abilities of the writer. I encourage you to use the book in this manner, working the chapters in order. In this way students will indeed gain hands-on knowledge of the different canons of rhetoric (invention, disposition, etc.) and the different modes of argument (logos, ethos, pathos), as well as different genres and their particular features.

You will also notice that, continuing the carpentry metaphor, part 2 is "Precision Tools and Finer Crafts," not "A Finished Building." I make no claim that this book can teach all there is to know about writing, or that learning to produce a clever imitation or parody of someone else's writing is the goal of the book. In pre-modern eras, a "masterpiece" was not the artist's greatest work, but the first piece produced by an apprentice showing him capable of becoming a "master" of the trade and setting up shop on his own. What I have tried to produce is a method by which students can come to their own voices, their own writing, and be ready to hang up their own shingles as accomplished users of complex prose. Thus the goal of the entire book is to get the students to the Afterword, "Setting Up Shop for Yourself," where I encourage the students to take what they have learned and move out on their own while giving them practical advice for how to do so.

Assessing Students' Progress

Because these assignments are quite different from what students are accustomed to doing in their writing classes, and because imitation—and the deeper learning that comes from it—proceeds in my experience not in a linear fashion but by quantum leaps after struggling and difficulty, I encourage you to find flexible ways of assessing and grading these assignments. A student who may on the first attempt completely miss obvious and fundamental features of some writing (the medieval style of salutation on a letter, Joyce's associative style in stream-of-consciousness narration) may then turn in a stunning piece of writing upon revision, as form and content come together after more careful analysis. Therefore, I recommend early and extensive feedback *without* grades, then waiting for revision before assessing final grades on the assignments. Portfolio grading works quite well for the assignments in this book for obvious reasons.

Parody and Tone

An imitation is not necessarily a parody, though it can be. *Native Son* and *Things Fall Apart* imitate classical Greek tragedies (albeit in prose) but are not parodies of them. Thus I am not suggesting that you merely ask your students to parody the voices, genres, structures, and forms I have provided here. Imitation can, and in most cases is, serious, sincere, and deeply challenging. Yet I am also aware that parody, performed well, is intellectually challenging, and can be a marvelous entry into the skill, ideology, and art of an accomplished writer. A well-accomplished parody—Jonathan Swift's "A Modest Proposal" comes to mind—can often highlight the conventions of discourse that otherwise might have remained hidden to the student. As a teacher, you will have to determine what you will allow and what you will not in the students' imitations. I myself have varied and learned in this regard. At times I have been much more lighthearted and playful in teaching these texts and exercises and have encouraged a great deal of parody; at other times I have wished my students to enter into a deep sympathy with the writers and take the assignments in all seriousness. In doing so I have realized the pitfalls of parody and lightheartedness in the classroom and have moved towards a more serious tone while, I hope, not losing my lightheartedness completely. I encourage you to try both and develop your own voice as you teach this text.

Challenging Assignments with Positive Results

These assignments are challenging, no doubt. But I wish to assure you of one thing: all of these assignments have been repeatedly field-tested in many different kinds of classrooms, from introductory composition at a virtually open-admissions college to advanced composition at a Greats Books-influenced, very selective private university. The assignments can work very well, and as the student examples will show you, even Cicero, as daunting as he may appear at first, is accessible and manageable by almost all levels of students.

I make no apologies for the challenging nature of these assignments. These sample texts provide a view into what accomplished writers actually *do* in a much more helpful way, I believe, than other composition texts on the market. And I believe that the movement to incorporate more serious writing, more literature, more creative nonfiction of all types, into the composition class can only have a salutary effect on students and their writing. For it is the kind of truism so obvious that one struggles to understand how it has become lost in the modern composition classroom: students only make real progress as writers, especially at the higher ends, by absorbing enormous amounts of excellent writing, by training their ears, eyes, hands, and minds on a diet of significant, complex, fascinating prose and poetry, writing that will nourish, challenge, stimulate, and inspire.

There are some, therefore, who might wish that my selections had been even more extensive, that each selection of Dickens or Joyce had been longer. There are times when I have wished the same, knowing, as I do now more than ever, that only long and extensive reading provides the background for good writing. But time and space—not just of the book, but of the classroom—limit what one can do, even in an Advanced Composition class, and I am producing a guide, not an anthology. Furthermore, as I believe you will see as you work through the exercises with your students, I preferred to have shorter selections which you and the students could analyze carefully, fully, and deeply, and which the students could then imitate with the same care, rather than heave a huge passage towards the students that would necessarily leave only a limited time for careful analysis. The selections do lengthen as I progress through the book. For those who would prefer longer, or different, selections, I counsel patience; I hope to follow this text with a reader that will contain more (and longer) selections that will be keyed to the exercises in the chapters here.

I furthermore know that the book is challenging to you, the instructor, as well: I ask a great deal of you. But I do not leave you alone. My comments in the Teacher's Notes help you work through the assignments in order, and I encourage you to take advantage of the experiences from different kinds of classrooms represented in the advice given there. I have found that teaching this way is challenging indeed, but the rewards are well worth the effort. I have for some time been engaged in a kind of Diogenean search for a teacher who actually enjoys grading papers, who attacks this crucial and time-consuming part of our vocation with enjoyment, even relish. I cannot say my lamp has found him or her yet, but I will say that grading these imitation assignments has been more enjoyable than any other grading I have done.

Part One: Foundations

Chapter One

Voices of the Senses:
Learning How to Describe

As I promised in the preface, and in my notes to the student and to the teacher, I am going to take you, immediately, in a different direction than most writing textbooks take you: imitating others' writing—their word choices, structures, and syntax—to help you develop writing skills and develop your own distinctive voice.

This imitation may seem strange at first, but it is the way most writers learn to write. In fact, it is the way most of us learn to do anything. Babies learn to speak by imitating their parents' voices, inflections, and syntactical structures. Athletes learn the skills of their sport by watching a coach do a move, then imitating it over and over until they "get it." Musicians, too, imitate. You might think that jazz musicians, for instance, with their free "improvising," just make things up as they go along. That's partly true, but you might not realize this: many of the greatest jazz musicians take the time to carefully, painstakingly, write out and memorize every note of the great solos of Louis Armstrong, Charlie Parker, and Dizzy Gillespie, among others. That is, their "free" improvisation develops from constant imitation of their models, their heroes, until they learn their "moves," their standard gestures. Writers, too, learn by imitating. In school, William Shakespeare and John Milton were given assignments asking them to imitate carefully the great Latin authors Ovid, Cicero, and others. Abraham Lincoln, surely the best writer of all our presidents, learned his prose style by imitating his great masters. But even ordinary people learned this way. If you have ever seen Ken Burns's PBS series on the Civil War, you heard letters written in beautiful prose by men and women with no more than a grammar-school education. How did they learn to write that way? Through practice—and imitation. In an age before telephones, the only way to communicate with friends more than a few miles away was by letter, so people back then wrote a great many more letters than we do now. And they learned prose style from the reading they did, or heard read aloud (since, before television, fireside reading and public debates were fundamental sources of entertainment).

So it is through imitation—through modeling others' voices—that you will develop your own distinctive voice and style, your own intelligent writing. You learn by imitating the structure of others' writing.

Let us begin with a task that at first seems simple and then often is distressingly difficult: description. One of the fundamental tasks of writing is to *describe*—to use words to render the world around you so others, those who are not with you at present, can see what you are seeing, hear what you are hearing, smell and even taste what you are smelling and tasting. You might have tried to do this in a letter, or an email, using words to describe something you saw, an event you experienced, or a person you met. You may also have found how difficult it can be: your words simply did not convey what you were trying to get across, and you ended up frustrated and annoyed. Yet description is crucial to almost any writing, and good description can enhance almost any kind of writing. If you can present your world, your experiences, to others, you can capture your readers' attention, help them understand what you are conveying, and develop a richer experience of the world. And it is important for you, too: if you can describe well, you enrich your own experience of the world, by paying attention to the details and textures and structures of your life. If you walk into, for instance, St. Peter's Basilica in Rome, and your only *language* for that experience is, "Oh, wow, this is, like, amazing!" then I would suggest you are not able to have as significant an experience of that church as someone who can describe the vast space, the swirling baroque architecture and sculpture, the glittering mosaics, the massive columns and piers, the odd changes in perspective, that are parts of one of the most important churches in the world. So learning description is not just a side skill for those who want to write poetry or short stories; it is perhaps *the* fundamental skill of all writing.

Perhaps the most difficult thing to do is to describe another person. Humans are so complex, so idiosyncratic—how can you possibly convey a person on the page? Just to convey someone's physical appearance is difficult enough, but to convey one person's haughtiness, another's timid uncertainty, or even the fluctuations between the two, can seem overwhelming at first.

There are typical "cookbook" instructions out there in other books that purport to teach you how to describe. I prefer that you learn by doing, by imitating some of the great writers who can render a person on the page. So I am going to take you through imitating others' ways of describing a person and have you learn and develop from those experiences some skills of description.

In this chapter, like all the ones to come, you will learn by doing. I will not at first explain to you everything you should find in the readings, or everything you should do in your imitation. You need to try things yourself first, and then, through revising the imitation, discover more. You should do all of the exercises carefully and to the best of your ability. The learning comes from the *doing*, not from listening to me, or to your professor lecture in class.

As you do these exercises, try to have a spirit of risk-taking. Take some chances. Don't be afraid to do something that might seem at first strange and unusual.

Task 1.1

Write one page describing someone you know. It can be a friend, a family member, a professor, the odd guy down the street, anyone. Just spend several paragraphs trying to capture this person in words.[1]

૨૭

When you are done, bring the description to class. Share it with two classmates. Explore what you did. What subject did you choose? Ask partners how well they can "see" this person, and what details help them to do so. What have you left out of the description, now that you read it aloud? What did you not capture about the person? Together with your partners, try to analyze your piece. How did you set up the description? What did you do first, second, and third? Did you try to build up to one particular feature, or did you start off with it? What sort of language did you use to convey your description—was it simple and direct, or complex and difficult? Reflect on the process of writing the description: did you find it difficult or easy? Which parts were easy and which were difficult? In your notebook, write one or two pages about this writing experience and what you learned from it.

Task 1.2

Read, slowly and carefully, the selection below from Geoffrey of Vinsauf's *Poetria Nova*. It will help to read it out loud, and I strongly recommend this. If there are words you have not encountered, look up their meanings. Take notes on the reading:

First, put in your own words what Geoffrey is saying.

Second, note the interesting ways he goes about saying these things. What structures does he employ? That is, in what order does he put the description, and what does he include? What does he leave out?

Some background before you read:

This excerpt is from the "New Poetry" or "New Poetics," which dates from the thirteenth century and was one of the most popular and well-known guides to writing in its day. Geoffrey's guide was intended to teach people how to write poetry. Most of the writers of the later Middle Ages knew this work; Geoffrey Chaucer, who wrote the *Canterbury Tales*, uses it, imitates it, and even makes fun of it in the "Nun's Priest's Tale." To Geoffrey of Vinsauf, description is a crucial skill; he says it is "the food and ample refreshment of the mind" and writers must "let it be . . . wise, let it also be both lengthy and lovely" (36). Here he is giving advice about how to describe a person, specifically how to describe a woman, and gives this example of how it should be done.[2]

Let the compass of Nature first fashion a sphere for her head; let the colour of gold give a glow to her hair, and lilies bloom high on her brow. Let her eyebrows resemble in dark beauty the blackberry, and a lovely and milk-white path separate their twin arches. Let her nose be straight, of moderate length, not too long nor too short for perfection. Let her eyes, those watch-fires of her brow, be radiant with emerald light, or with the brightness of stars. Let her countenance emulate dawn: not red, nor yet white—but at once neither of those colors and both. Let her mouth be bright, small in shape—as it were, a half-circle. Let her lips be rounded and full, but moderately so; let them glow, aflame, but with gentle fire. Let her teeth be snowy, regular, all of one size, and her breath like the fragrance of incense. Smoother than polished marble let Nature fashion her chin—Nature, so potent a sculptor. Let her neck be a precious column of milk-white beauty, holding high the perfection of her countenance. From her crystal throat let radiance gleam, to enchant the eye of the viewer and enslave his heart. Let her shoulders, conforming to beauty's law, not slope in unlovely descent, nor jut out with an awkward rise: rather, let them be gracefully straight. Let her arms be a joy to behold, charming in their grace and their length. Let soft and slim loveliness, a form shapely and white, a line long and straight, flow into her slender fingers. Let her breast, the image of snow, show side by side its twin virginal gems. Let her waist be close girt, and so slim that a hand may encircle it. For the other parts I am silent—here the mind's speech is more apt than the tongue's. Let her leg be of graceful length and her wonderfully tiny foot dance with joy at its smallness.[3]

Task 1.3

Now, take your description from Task 1.1 and rewrite it, imitating the style and structure of Geoffrey of Vinsauf's description. Try to imitate the style of the medieval description, from the overarching head-to-toe structure to some of the unusual phrasing to the comparisons through simile and metaphor. Look at individual sentences and try to imitate their structure and vocabulary.[4]

To perform this assignment, you will need to return to and re-read the medieval description very carefully as you write. (This careful re-reading, and even re-re-reading, can be one of the most beneficial aspects of these assignments.) You'll have to look at the large and small ways that this "voice" is created.

> Look at the macrostructure of Geoffrey's style; that is, notice the large blocks of structure that set up this voice. Then look further: what does Geoffrey consciously and conspicuously omit? Why do you think he does this?

> Look at the microstructure of Geoffrey's style. What little turns of phrase make this voice sound as it does? What sort of diction (that is, word choice or vocabulary) makes this sound so different? Are the sentences long and ornate, or are they short and concise? Are they full of similes and images and metaphors, or are they straightforward and flat? Does the writing refer to or allude to other writings? What other little things make up the sound of this voice? Try to do what those things do.[5]

All writing has this combination of macrostructure and microstructure—the large blocks of thought and how the writer lays them out, and the small features of each sentence (or the pattern of sentences). This is how voice comes about, though there can often be various microstructure voices within the same macrostructure.

ও

Bring the descriptions to class. Read them aloud to classmates. Which features did you capture that your partners did not? Are there some things your partners noticed and were able to capture that you were not able to capture?[26]

Here is an example from a student, Stephanie Duarte. Watch how well she captures the features Geoffrey includes in his description.

Let God initially create an oval for his head; let sunlight emanate rays into his hair. Let his eyebrows, golden and soft, resemble a soft peach's fur. Let his nose be small and so perfectly rounded. Let his eyes, the sapphires of his brow, shimmer with a cerulean ocean gleam, or with the intensity of the morning sky. Let his visage convey the heavens; not silver, nor yet gold—yet still both. Let his mouth be dazzling and small—as it were, elliptic. Let his lips be thin yet plump; let their pinkness burn like the gentle burn of the pink moonlight. Let his teeth be white, straight, aligned perfectly, and his breath like the sweetness of mint leaves. More defined than a chiseled statue let God create his chin—God, such a marvelous creator. Let his neck be a soft and creamy pillar, holding his flawless visage. From his muscular throat let attractiveness beam into the gaze of the spectator and ensnare her love. Let his shoulders, remaining consistent with the rules of beauty, not appear gaunt and bony, nor protrude in heftiness: rather, let them be handsomely strapping. Let his arms be exciting to watch, enticing with their well-built appeal. Let hard and strong attractiveness, a form pleasing, angled impeccably, surge down into his manly

9

fingers. Let his chest, the essence of pulchritude, show its juxtaposed pectorals. Let his waist be tantalizing and firm so that a hand may wish to caress it. For the further parts I shall remain taciturn; here only the imagination can unzip the hidden wonders. Let his leg be of seductive form and his magnificently large foot stir rhythmically to unheard music.

You will notice a few times that Ms. Duarte's inability to perform the assignment with complete seriousness sneaks into her comparisons (especially, perhaps, in the modesty *topos?*). She seems to be skirting the land between imitation and parody here. But she is learning to use words and to describe in new ways, and in fact, her attraction to this man comes through amidst the ornate description. As she herself noted, she had never been asked to write like this before, and it felt like stretching new muscles. And it took her a couple of revisions to get this piece to this point. Imitating Geoffrey's style—something she is, of course, unlikely to need or want to do in a contemporary writing situation—gave her new ways to conceive of describing this man, and new rhetorical skills as well.

A brief word about plagiarism and imitation:

Plagiarism—stealing someone else's ideas and words and pretending that they are yours—is wrong. In fact, it is one of the worst sins you can commit in an academic community. Why is this so? Well, in a very simple sense, it is because you are stealing someone else's hard work. If you do not know now how much hard work it is to write something, to get the phrasing just right, to choose just the perfect word to convey your ideas, you soon will. And you will soon be enraged at the idea of someone taking *your* words and passing them off as his own. But more than that, plagiarism steals what is most internal, precious, and individual to us: our thoughts, our concepts, our notions about the world. If you are unsure about what constitutes plagiarism, meet with your writing instructor and discuss this matter.

But what about imitation? Isn't this plagiarism? If a jazz musician borrows a riff from Charlie Parker, isn't that plagiarism? If a hip-hop group samples a riff from another song, doesn't that violate copyright? These are difficult issues, and not everyone agrees on them. But I might suggest a difference in the notion that plagiarism just steals and falsely tries to represent (that is, re-present) the words and ideas as if they were one's own, whereas, in imitation, we borrow *and adapt* to form something new, in a new context, in a new way.

Right now, we are merely engaging in an exercise: you will not be using Geoffrey's words and presenting them as if they are your own; you are handing in an exercise specifically designated as an imitation. So for now, I am asking you to trust me: you won't be charged with plagiarism for writing too closely to Geoffrey of Vinsauf's words.

Understanding plagiarism is crucial, especially in academic discourse, where we are required more strictly than in any other discourse to list and cite our sources. And again, if you or your instructor wish to have a more lengthy discussion about this issue at this point, do so by all means. But just for these imitation exercises—which you do not intend to publish or publicly present—I want to encourage you to imitate and adapt, and (again, just for these exercises) not worry too much about plagiarism. The point of imitation is to borrow, to mimic, in the service of learning how another's voice works and can shape your writing. And you can't do that without using some of the phrases, images, and sentence structures from the model you are imitating. If you are really stuck here, just start by using the exact sentence structures in the description and plugging in words that relate to the person you are describing. Soon you'll get the idea and start to more freely imitate the voice on your own. And as we proceed, you can study and learn more about plagiarism.

ટ✦

Now we're going to take that description and move it from the Middle Ages into more recent times. You will now revise it into a different shape by imitating one of the great masters of description, Charles Dickens. Dickens was both a popular and a critical success with such novels as *A Tale of Two Cities* and *Hard Times*, and he was remarkable for his ability to sketch a character in a short space.

Task 1.4

Read the description of Magwitch from Charles Dickens's *Great Expectations*. Again, read carefully, and try to see how Dickens builds up these characters.

Some background before you read:

This selection is from the very beginning—the exposition—of Dickens' novel, where he is getting the characters "on stage" for his story. Pip, the little boy telling the story, is an orphan; he has just described how he has been wandering in the marshes near his home in southeast England. He has come upon a graveyard and has realized that the people buried there are his mother, father, and siblings, and that "the small bundle of shivers growing afraid of it all and beginning to cry, was Pip." At this point a man "started up from among the graves" and threatens to cut Pip's throat unless he keeps still. (We later find out that this man is the convict Magwitch.) Pip describes him in this way:

A fearful man, all in coarse grey, with a great iron on his leg. A man with no hat, and with broken shoes, and with an old rag tied round his head. A man who had been soaked in water, and smothered in mud, and lamed by stones, and cut by flints, and stung by nettles, and torn by briars; who limped, and shivered, and glared and growled; and whose teeth chattered in his head as he seized me by the chin.[7]

Task 1.5

Now revise your description from Task 1.3, putting it in the style and voice of this selection from Charles Dickens. Try to describe your subject the way Dickens would have.

When you are done, bring the description to class and share it with a partner. What aspects were you able to capture from the model? Which ones did you neglect that your partner caught? More importantly, how did describing your subject in this way differ from describing the person using Geoffrey as a model? What were you forced to leave out? Were you able to convey things that you were not able to convey before? What differences do you see in these two modes of description? What have you learned about description by doing this?

Here is Stephanie Duarte's description based on the Dickens example:

A rugged man, all in an ashen ensemble, with a heavy metal cane at his side. A man with a tattered cap, and with ragged moccasins, and with a shabby handkerchief fastened around his dirty neck. A man who had been drenched in rainfall, and exposed to snow, and crippled by ice, and slashed by barbs, and penetrated by mosquitoes, and mangled by cactus; who hobbled, and trembled, and frowned and snarled; and whose lips quivered as he caught me by the face.

You might look back to Ms. Duarte's first description to see how differently this one works. Which do you find more effective, and why?

Task 1.6

Next, read the description of Mrs. Joe from just a few pages later in the same novel. Again, notice macrostructure and microstructure: how does Dickens build this description? What techniques does he use? What does he do first, second, then third?

A bit more background before you read:

Here, at the beginning of chapter 2, Dickens shows us Pip's domestic situation. His parents dead, he lives with a sister much older than he and with her husband, Joe Gargery. Joe is one of the kindest, sweetest characters in all of literature; Pip's sister, "Mrs. Joe," is, as you will see, a different sort. We never learn the first name of Pip's sister; she is always "Mrs. Joe Gargery." You might consider why Dickens does this and how it contributes to her description.

My sister, Mrs. Joe Gargery, was more than twenty years older than I, and had established a great reputation with herself and the neighbours because she had brought me up "by hand." Having at that time to find out for myself what the expression meant, and knowing her to have a hard and heavy hand, and to be much in the habit of laying it upon her husband as well as upon me, I supposed that Joe Gargery and I were both brought up by hand.

She was not a good-looking woman, my sister; and I had a general impression that she must have made Joe Gargery marry her by hand. Joe was a fair man, with curls of flaxen hair on each side of his smooth face, and with eyes of such a very undecided blue that they seemed to have somehow got mixed with their own whites. He was a mild, good-natured, sweet-tempered, easygoing, foolish, dear fellow—a sort of Hercules in strength, and also in weakness.

My sister, Mrs. Joe, with black hair and eyes, had such a prevailing redness of skin that I sometimes used to wonder whether it was possible she washed herself with a nutmeg-grater instead of soap. She was tall and bony, and almost always wore a coarse apron, fastened over her figure behind with two loops, and having a square impregnable bib in front, that was stuck full of pins and needles. She made it a powerful merit in herself, and a strong reproach against Joe, that she wore this apron so much. Though I really see no reason why she should have worn it at all: or why, if she did wear it at all, she should not have taken it off, every day of her life.[8]

Task 1.7

Now, based on your analysis of this passage, revise your description further, putting it in the style of this description of Mrs. Joe and Joe Gargery. Watch how the form and the content change as you do so.

After you do so, again bring your assignment to class. Compare your work with others' descriptions and discuss the changes you made to the earlier description. What do you begin to discover about imitation, about how form and content are related, about syntax and word choice?

Here again is Stephanie Duarte's work; this time she has moved to describing a different set of people. Notice the features of Dickens' prose that she is able to capture. Are there things you might have done differently? I wouldn't call it perfect—comparing the violent and angry Achilles to her mild friend seems a little off—but she does a wonderful job with so many of the details that one can see Ms. Duarte improving as she imitates. Do you find this one more or less satisfying and effective than the other two attempts at description?

My friend, Mrs. Joshua Thompson to be, was my age, and had developed a strong status among our small society be-

cause she was "the boss." Having at that time to search for
the meaning of that phrase, and knowing her to dictate, and
to be in the habit of giving orders to her boyfriend as well as
me, I supposed that her boyfriend and I were both subordinate to the boss.

She was not an attractive girl, my friend, and I assumed
that she probably forced Joshua Thompson to date her by
strict orders from the boss. Joshua was a pale man, with
spikes of buzzed hair on every part of his smooth head, and
with eyes with a much washed-out green that they seemed
to have drowned within the whites of his eyes. He was a nice,
good-hearted, fine-humored, relaxed, friendly, dear lad—a
sort of Achilles in both power and flaw.

My friend, Mrs. Joshua Thompson to be, with blond hair
and blue eyes, had such chalky skin that I sometimes used
to question whether she ever stepped foot into the sunlight.
She was colossal and bulky, and almost always wore his big
baggy sweatpants, pulled up over her rear and drawn into a
knot at the drawstring. She incorporated these sweatpants
into her authority; they were a symbol of her tyranny that
she wore these pants constantly. Although I find no explanation as to why she ever needed to wear them: or why if she
ever wore them, she was unable ever to take them off.

Great Ideas: Charles Dickens, Impressionism, and Realism[9]

You may have found the description of Magwitch in particular
quite strange. Dickens has Pip notice only a few things about
Magwitch—his clothes, his shoes, his movements. How can this
be an adequate description? And yet you may have sensed that
Dickens conveys more about Magwitch than the more "complete" description Geoffrey created.

You might know that, during the time Dickens was writing, a group of French painters began a new movement in vi-
sual art called "Impressionism." These painters—among them

Monet, Renoir, Degas, and others—believed that, to be "realistic," one must paint only the actual impressions one sees, not what is "really there," that is, what your brain helps you conclude is "really there" from these sense impressions. You have surely seen Impressionist paintings: we get not each individual leaf of a tree, but the sparkling and shimmering of the sun as it dances off of the leaves. We get not the smooth surface of a river, but daring thick brush strokes representing the light playing off of the surface of the water. To the Impressionists, this was a "truer" way to paint, because it recorded what we actually see, not what our brains tell us is actually there. When you stand up close to an Impressionist painting, you see what appear to be only random globs of paint littering the canvas. It is only when you step back, across the room, that the vision appears, and you see boaters on a river, or lily pads on the water. And though their work was initially derided as ugly, and the official Academy refused to show their work, now these paintings are among the most well-known and most beloved of our day. The Impressionists taught us to see in a different way, and now it has become one of the ways we see.

You might now realize that Dickens is doing much the same in his description of Magwitch. Often in novels written around this time, when a character enters the scene, the author stops the action and gives a more or less "complete" description of the person. You've read novels like this: a character walks in the door, and we get an entire paragraph describing the character. Here in G. K. Chesterton's *The Man Who Was Thursday*, written after Dickens' work but really based on older forms, Chesterton stops the action to describe one of the characters (named Wednesday):

Next was Wednesday, a certain Marquis de St. Eustache, a sufficiently characteristic figure. The first few glances found nothing unusual about him, except that he was the only man at table who wore the fashionable clothes as if they were really his own. He had a black French beard cut square and a black English frock-coat cut even squarer. But Syme, sensitive to such things, felt somehow that the man carried a rich atmosphere with him, a rich atmosphere that suffocated. It reminded one irrationally of drowsy odours and of dying lamps in the darker poems of Byron and Poe. With this went a sense of his being clad, not in lighter colours, but in softer materials; his black seemed richer and warmer than the black shades about him, as if it were compounded of profound colour. His black coat looked as if it were only black by being too dense a purple. His black beard looked as if it were only black by being too deep a blue. And in the gloom and thickness of the beard his dark red mouth showed sensual and scornful. Whatever he was he was not a Frenchman; he might be a Jew; he might be something deeper yet in the dark heart of the East. In the bright coloured Persian tiles and pictures showing tyrants hunting, you may see just those almond eyes, those blue-black beards, those cruel, crimson lips.

Now Chesterton is a great writer in many ways, and has valuable, important things to say to us even today. But I would maintain—and I think he would, too—that Dickens is the superior novelist, has the superior skill at description. Notice how different from Dickens' description this is, how static it is. (You might also notice the antisemitism that Chesterton does not even bother to conceal.) Chesterton seems to believe that description itself is static, a set piece, something you get out of the way before going on with the narrative.

What Dickens was after was something different, something more like what the Impressionists were after. A convict grabs a terrified little boy; is it *realistic* that his description of the man would be rational, objective, and complete? No; what he would see would be quick impressions, necessarily fragmentary in nature. And so watch what happens: in the first sentence (actually a fragment, as Dickens suggests the fragmentary aspect of these impressions), Pip gets an immediate overall impression ("a fearful man"), then notices his clothes ("all in coarse grey"), and then looks down and notices the one detail that sums up everything ("with a great iron on his leg")—that is, Pip realizes that Magwitch is a convict. The description goes on from there, bouncing around to other impressions, but Dickens never adds them up for us; it is up to the reader to back off and put all of his brush strokes together into the coherent picture of Magwitch.

In other ways Dickens is not an especially "impression-istic" writer; the full realization of this technique would await later writers who led the way into modernism—writers like Stephen Crane and Joseph Conrad. Still, I hope you can see the contrast here, and the real challenge that Impressionism created in art. It began to ask seriously: what is "realism," and how best can one achieve an art that "really" reflects what one sees? Is it more "realistic" to be subjective? It is not my job to answer that question for you, but merely to have you see how it was asked, and the question's implications for writing. And to help you see that, in choosing Dickens for a role model, the Master to whom you apprentice, you engage in significant aesthetic questions while learning new techniques for your writing.

Task 1.8

Write for a few paragraphs, reflecting on what you've learned about description. How have this chapter and these assignments made you more aware of the methods we use to describe people? How has it improved your ability to describe people? How have the methods of description changed over the years?[10]

Why We're Doing This

One of the most powerful things you can do as a writer is to sketch a person in a few words so that others can "see" and "experience" that person. It's a core of much good writing. But as I hope you have discovered, it is not as easy as it looks. And in addition, the "right" way to describe a person has changed over time—a pretty interesting idea upon which you might meditate a bit. What would have counted for good description in, say, 1380 (Chaucer's time) may not have been seen as good description in Dickens' time, and vice versa. People are interested in different qualities, and structures in description do change. Therefore, one more piece of advice: do not think you have learned everything about description just by apprenticing yourself to Geoffrey and to Charles Dickens. If you want to improve your ability to describe people, read more great writers; learn from them; study their techniques of description, and then try to imitate them. We can only give you a small sample here in order to get you started, to stretch your writing muscles by having you take on different models and different tasks. We want you to see how things change when you imitate different models and try on different voices. But if you want to continue to improve, you will have to seek out more models, more masters to whom you can apprentice yourself—and then you will have to model upon them, study under their tutelage.[11]

But you're not likely to write in this style, right? So why do this? Simply this—the styles presented here are so different, the diction and phrasing so unusual to our ears today, that it is a good place to show you how a different voice and style, even in the simple exercise of description, can produce very different sorts of writing. The *task* did not change; throughout the chapter, you were doing the same thing that you did in Task 1.1—describing a person—yet look how different it now is. And I thought it would be so very different that you might have fun stretching, trying on a voice which would be very different from the one you usually use.

Furthermore, you really have to *think* in this different voice to write like Geoffrey or Dickens. You have to think like a medieval writer or a nineteenth-century novelist; you must feel as he feels, and think using his language. And that's the way it is in all writing. To write a good business letter, you have to think like a businessperson. To write a good novel, you have to think like a novelist—a William Faulkner or a James Joyce or a Eudora Welty. To write a good movie review, you have to think like Siskel and Ebert or Pauline Kael or Michael Medved. Learning to write by imitation is not just the process of faking someone else's words; it is the process of learning to *think* in different patterns.

Special Note to Students at the End of This First Chapter

This experience was probably quite different for you. You may not have ever seen writing like some of this before, much less tried to write like it. And that, of course, is precisely the point: I am asking you to "put on" a completely different voice than you have ever used before. In so doing, you stretch your "writing muscles" just like an athlete who tries a new way of throwing the ball, or like a violinist who tries a new bow technique. And in doing this, you will increase the stock of "voices" you have to draw upon in future writing situations. You say you'll never use this particular voice, right? That you'll never again write like a medieval poet, or a nineteenth-century novelist? That's okay. The simple fact that you have the experience of writing in a new voice will give you more flexibility and ability in any writing situation. And the experience of imitating a new voice will show you one way to deal with any new writing situation you find yourself in: you go find the kind of writing you want to do, and imitate the best of that kind of writing.

Extra Exercises for Those Who Want to Do More

Find writers whose descriptions you find particularly vivid. Use them as models, and try transforming your descriptions from this chapter into their voices. Use the same method you learned in this chapter—break down the model's macrostructure and microstructure, then attempt to imitate as many of those features as you can.

Whenever you have a few spare minutes—in a restaurant, waiting in line at the Department of Motor Vehicles, the five minutes before class starts—try describing some person around you. If you are not in a place where you can take out paper and pen, just do it in your head. Try different techniques—Geoffrey's, Dickens', others. This skill improves immediately with constant practice.

Chapter Two

Voices of Observation: Describing Actions, Making Meaning

*I*n chapter 1, you worked on observing, and then describing in words, a person. It was practice in paying attention; it was practice in taking what you had observed and finding the words with which to render that complex person so that others could experience him or her.[1] It was practice in imitating another's voice, style, diction, syntax.

But that description was, to a large extent, static. You attempted to take a kind of snapshot of a person, frozen in a single moment in time, and present it to the reader. Life, however, is rarely static; it is inherently dynamic. People walk, gesture, eat, swat at flies, react to stimuli. How, then, can we develop our descriptive abilities to convey actions, events, change?

Again, this is more difficult than it might at first appear— you may have felt the frustration as you tried to describe in an email what you did last night, or struggled with conveying the chaos of a car accident that you saw as a witness. And yet it is, as those two examples show, something we all do all the time, and must do, simply to take part in conversation with others, to relate our experiences, to convey, sometimes, our deepest concerns and ideas. The question is, how can we do it better? How can we render actions so that we make our readers see events as clearly as if they were watching a movie?

In this chapter you will again imitate masters of these skills, this time two of the great writers of Modernism, that powerful artistic movement of the first half of the twentieth century. You will again learn not through abstract rules, but by doing, by imitating, by trying yourself to mimic and accomplish what these writers discovered on their own.

As before, we will start with a warm-up exercise that will give us our subject matter. First, we need to find some events, some actions, that we can practice describing.

Task 2.1

Find and read the minutes of a meeting. It could be a club meeting, a committee meeting, or any other type of meeting. It would be very good if this were a meeting you yourself had attended, so you know what happened and can remember details. If you cannot find any minutes, expand your notion of "meeting"—it could be some people getting together to discuss something, or an activity at your church, or a sporting event. If all of this fails you, make up a meeting and make up the minutes for it.[2]

Bring your minutes to class. Read them to partners in your group. You will soon discover that minutes are not terribly descriptive; they tend to boil down the events of the meeting into their barest details: what motions were introduced, what actions were taken, some brief summary of the debates on the various issues. So what you need to do is try to recall more of the detail that a set of minutes leaves out. Take turns asking one another about details of the meeting: why did that happen? What did she say, exactly? What was he wearing? Did she seem angry, or just exasperated? Try to help one another remember as many of the tangible details of the meeting as possible. You might also look for the interesting moments of the meeting—were there particular times of tension, of drama, of emotion? When you are done, make some notes recording these details. When you have a quiet moment, close your eyes and imagine you are again sitting in the meeting; try to play it in your mind like a movie. Record any further details that you now remember.

Task 2.2

Read the following short story, "A Day's Wait," by Ernest Hemingway, slowly and carefully. As you read, try to figure out what makes Hemingway's voice so distinctive, and how he is able to make you "see" the story in your head.[3]

Some background before you read:

Hemingway was once one of the most important figures in American literature, a novelist who was simultaneously popular and artistically respected. He was born in Chicago and left after high school to be a reporter for the *Kansas City Star*; his early career in journalism seems to have shaped his style. He served in World War I as an ambulance driver, was wounded, and wrote of this period often, gaining his fame with novels like *The Sun Also Rises* (1926) and *A Farewell to Arms* (1929). He later covered the Spanish Civil War and World War II even while continuing to write novels. After the Second World War he was a celebrity; his drinking, his love of fishing and big-game hunting were followed closely in the press. Hemingway's strikingly male, even macho fictional world is not so much in fashion these days, but his war novels were early explorations of the devastation war wreaks on men, and his spare style—probably his greatest achievement—has been imitated and adapted by many writers since. He took his own life in 1961. The following story, "A Day's Wait," was published in the mature stage of his career, in 1938, and is somewhat uncharacteristic in that it concerns a domestic, family scene: a boy is sick, and his father tries to comfort him, but the boy becomes terrified because he makes a simple mistake.

He came into the room to shut the windows while we were still in bed and I saw he looked ill. He was shivering, his face was white, and he walked slowly as though it ached to move.

"What's the matter, Schatz?"

"I've got a headache."

"You better go back to bed."

"No, I'm all right."

"You go to bed. I'll see you when I'm dressed."

But when I came downstairs he was dressed, sitting by the fire, looking a very sick and miserable boy of nine years. When I put my hand on his forehead I knew he had a fever.

"You go up to bed," I said, "you're sick."

"I'm all right," he said.

When the doctor came he took the boy's temperature.

"What is it?" I asked him.

"One hundred and two."

Downstairs, the doctor left three different medicines in different colored capsules with instructions for giving them. One was to bring down the fever, another a purgative, the third to overcome an acid condition. The germs of influenza can only exist in an acid condition, he explained. He seemed to know all about influenza and said there was nothing to worry about if the fever did not go above one hundred and four degrees. This was a light epidemic of flu and there was no danger if you avoided pneumonia.

Back in the room I wrote the boy's temperature down and made a note of the time to give the various capsules.

"Do you want me to read to you?"

"All right. If you want to," said the boy. His face was very white and there were dark areas under his eyes. He lay still in the bed and seemed very detached from what was going on.

I read aloud from Howard Pyle's *Book of Pirates;* but I could see he was not following what I was reading.

"How do you feel, Schatz?" I asked him.

"Just the same so far," he said.

I sat at the foot of the bed and read to myself while I waited for it to be time to give another capsule. It would have been natural for him to go to sleep, but when I looked up he was looking at the foot of the bed, looking very strangely.

"Why don't you try to go to sleep? I'll wake you for the medicine."

"I'd rather stay awake."

After a while he said to me, "You don't have to stay in here with me, Papa, if it bothers you."

"It doesn't bother me."

"No, I mean you don't have to stay if it's going to bother you."

I thought perhaps he was a little lightheaded and after giving him the prescribed capsules at eleven o'clock I went out for a while.

It was a bright, cold day, the ground covered with a sleet that had frozen so that it seemed as if all the bare trees, the bushes, the cut brush, and all the grass and the bare ground had been varnished with ice. I took the young Irish setter for a little walk up the road and along a frozen creek, but it was difficult to stand or walk on the glassy surface and the red dog slipped and slithered and I fell twice, hard, once dropping my gun and having it slide away over the ice.

We flushed a covey of quail under a high clay bank with overhanging brush and I killed two as they went out of sight over the top of the bank. Some of the covey lit in trees, but most of them scattered into brush piles and it was necessary to jump on the ice-coated mounds of brush several times before they would flush. Coming out while you were poised unsteadily on the icy, springy brush they made difficult shooting and I killed two, missed five, and started back pleased to have found a covey close to the house and happy there were so many left to find on another day.

At the house they said the boy had refused to let any one come into the room.

"You can't come in," he said. "You mustn't get what I have."

I went up to him and found him in exactly the position I had left him, white-faced, but with the tops of his cheeks flushed by the fever, staring still, as he had stared, at the foot of the bed.

I took his temperature.

"What is it?"

"Something like a hundred," I said. It was one hundred and two and four tenths.

"It was a hundred and two," he said.

"Who said so?"

"The doctor."

"Your temperature is all right," I said. "It's nothing to worry about."

"I don't worry," he said, "but I can't keep from thinking."

"Don't think," I said. "Just take it easy."

"I'm taking it easy," he said and looked straight ahead. He was evidently holding tight onto himself about something.

"Take this with water."

"Do you think it will do any good?"

"Of course it will."

I sat down and opened the *Pirate* book and commenced to read, but I could see he was not following, so I stopped.

"About what time do you think I'm going to die?" he asked.

"What?"

"About how long will it be before I die?"

"You aren't going to die. What's the matter with you?"

"Oh, yes, I am. I heard him say a hundred and two."

"People don't die with a fever of one hundred and two. That's a silly way to talk."

"I know they do. At school in France the boys told me you can't live with forty-four degrees. I've got a hundred and two."

He had been waiting to die all day, ever since nine o'clock in the morning.

"You poor Schatz," I said. "Poor old Schatz. It's like miles and kilometers. You aren't going to die. That's a different thermometer. On that thermometer thirty-seven is normal. On this kind it's ninety-eight."

"Are you sure?"

"Absolutely," I said. "It's like miles and kilometers. You know, like, how many kilometers we make when we do seventy miles in the car?"

"Oh," he said.

But his gaze at the foot of the bed relaxed slowly. The hold over himself relaxed too, finally, and the next day it was very slack and he cried very easily at little things that were of no importance.

Task 2.3

Now, take the minutes from Task 2.1 and rewrite them, casting them in Hemingway's style. Try to capture the way Hemingway relates the events of this one day with actions, dialogue, and description. Pay attention to Hemingway's *word choice*, or diction. Look at the syntax of his sentences and try to imitate that as well.[4]

To complete this assignment, you'll have to go back and re-read the story very carefully as you write. (This careful re-reading, and even re-re-reading, can be one of the most beneficial aspects of these assignments.) You'll have to look at the large and small ways that this "voice" is created.[5]

Look at the macrostructure of Hemingway's style; that is, notice the large blocks of structure that set up this voice. How and when does he begin the story—that is, how does he handle the exposition? What does he narrate next? How does the story add complications to drive the narrative forward? Where does he slow down time, describing things in great detail, and where does he skim over a great deal of time? How does he end the story—with a large climax or something else?[6]

Look at the microstructure of Hemingway's style. Start with length and syntax of his sentences: are they long and complex, or short and simple? Are they full of similes and images and metaphors, or are they straightforward and flat? What little turns of phrase make this voice sound as it does? What sort of diction (that is, word choice or vocabulary) makes this sound so different? How does Hemingway create dialogue that seems real? What other

29

little things make up the sound of this voice? Try to do what those things do.[7]

All writing has this combination of macrostructure and microstructure—the large blocks of thought and how they are laid out, and the small features of each sentence (or the pattern of sentences). This is how voice comes about, though there can often be various microstructure voices within the same macrostructure.

Bring your completed imitation to class, and share it with a partner or two. What did you fail to capture that your partners were able to imitate? What features did you imitate that they did not? How did this rewriting change the minutes you began with? Discuss these things, and then take some notes for revising your description of the meeting.

Interlude: Description, the Five Senses, and "Showing" vs. "Telling"

Many of us are told from an early age that the way to make our writing more descriptive is to "use lots of adjectives." But in reality, piled-up adjectives do not work very well when we are trying to describe. "She was angry." "He was a belligerent, annoying twerp." "The executive was domineering but kindly, impatient but forgiving." According to what we are often told, that should be good descriptive writing. But it does not work, for the most part; it does not help us see the executive, really. Why? Because when we use an adjective, the reader supplies in his head a picture of "belligerent" from his own memory—perhaps a time when a friend was belligerent, or his cousin, or his boss. But that's not what you want, right? You want him to see *this* executive, this unique person, being belligerent. So you cannot simply "tell" that the person was angry, or impatient, or forgiving.

Instead, you must *show*. That is, rather than *telling* the resulting mental understanding (belligerence), you must reproduce the sense data that entered into your brain that day . . . and let the readers' brains come to the conclusion that the person was angry, or impatient, or whatever.

Try this. Get with a partner. Close your eyes and imagine you have just driven home, walked in the door, and found your mother standing there, really *angry*. Got the image? Okay, now, SHOW her to us. If you have any experience with her what-soever, and your mother is really angry, it doesn't take but an instant to realize she is angry, right? So show just what you see: what are her eyes doing? (What color are her eyes?) What is she doing with her hands? Does she tap her fingers? (Does she wear rings? What do they look like?) How does she move her mouth—or doesn't she? (Gesture is crucial in conveying mood and meaning, as the folks who write books in Non-Verbal Com-munication tell us.) Is she standing or sitting? Instruct your partner to continue asking you for *sensory input*, and not adjec-tives that explain that input. Then expand. What do you hear? Perhaps your mother gets quiet when she is angry. You think you can't describe silence? Yes, you can; tell us what you *hear*—the sound of the roast sizzling in the oven, the washing machine, the radio playing in the back room (which song? What parts of the chorus? Be specific!), the dog (which breed?) barking three doors down the street—*that* will emphasize the silence in the room where you are standing. Use all five senses—describe the texture of the La-Z-Boy on which you are resting your hand. What do you smell? After you have done this, put the scene in motion: what happens next? Who says what? Who moves where in the room?[8]

The goal here is for your partner to take in the same sen-sory information you received when you stood in the room that day. If you can do that, you won't need to *tell* your partners "My mother was angry"; they'll get it. Hemingway did not invent good description, but through his terse style, he is a good model for learning it, for he sticks to it almost relentlessly.

ॠ

Here is an example of a student, Christi Urash, who took a sim-ple meeting and modified it by imitating Hemingway. See what you can learn from her efforts. Notice how she did a fine job with "showing" to create the sense impressions that we might have received had we been at the meeting. She does not tell us the emotions of the meeting, but instead shows us what happened so we can experience the emotions along with her. It also helps description if it comes from a specific point of view—we must look out through someone's eyes, hear with her ears, rather than floating above the action as a God-like third-person observer. You might see things that you did not capture in your Hemingway imitation that now are more obvious; conversely, you might have imitated in Hemingway some things that Ms. Urash missed.

He was not my favorite person. He demanded way too much from all of us. He expected our work on time. The only acceptable excuse was death. I needed to talk to him and I was not looking forward to it. I walked toward his office planning my brilliant argument. I just caught him walking out to his car.

"Excuse me, sir."

His face told me he was not pleased to see me.

"Yes, Miss Urash?"

"I'm so glad I caught you. I really need to speak to you about my paper."

"Yes?"

This was the point when my genius was supposed to kick in. My sweet innocent face would appeal to his humanity. I was sure he would have pity on me. One more day was all I needed. I forgot my speech.

"I was hoping you could find it in your heart to understand. I ran into problems with my research."

"Really? The paper is due tomorrow, you know?"

"Uh, yes sir. I do know."

"Well?"

"Well sir, here's the thing. I found some information about Sir Francis Drake that changes my whole thesis."

"Okay. So?"

"I don't think I can have fifteen pages for you by tomorrow. I'm having to rethink the whole thing."

"Well, you can do it. You just have to work hard."

"I was hoping you would let me have more time. I need to do well on this paper. I don't think it will be a good paper by tomorrow."

"Do your best. That's all I can tell you. I expect your paper at the start of class tomorrow. I don't accept late work."

I fumbled for something to change his mind. If I could just make him understand. He walked away while my mind searched desperately. I had nothing.

I returned to my apartment across from campus to begin my paper. I was going to do my best to finish. I had chosen to write about my ancestor Sir Francis Drake. I didn't like him very much that day. Months of preparation all confused by one last minute search on the Internet. I filled my glass with Coke and I set the bottle on my desk. I opened a bag of cherry flavored, pull-n-peel licorice ropes and popped open a can of Pringles. It was going to be a long night.

I worked through the night. I only stopped to refill my glass or to go to the bathroom. I finished writing around six in the morning. I was sure I could type it up by class at ten. I'm a slow typer and I had forgotten to plan time for internal citations. Half an hour before class I was one page from finishing.

What happened then was nuts. I didn't believe it when it happened. At twenty-eight minutes to ten my electricity went out. My computer screen went black and my mind went blank. Shock set in. I sat there staring at the screen for a long time. I had forgotten to save after page six.

I finally thought to call the apartment office. If it was a widespread problem he might understand.

"Hello? Tower Village Apartments."

"Hi, this is Christi Urash in number 2045."

"How can I help you, Miss Urash?"

"My electricity went out a few minutes ago. I was wondering if everybody else's was out."

"No one else has called and we have no problem here. You should call the electric company to report the problem."

"Okay, thanks."

I called the company and they said their computers did show a problem in my area. They would send someone right out. It was limited to my building so it was probably just our outside fuse box. I'm not sure what else was said. I had stopped paying attention after "just your building."

My story had just gotten more unbelievable.

I didn't go to class. I curled up on my couch and slept until evening. I had gotten a sixty-eight on my mid-term exam. The paper was worth twenty-five percent of my grade. He didn't accept late papers. There was nothing I could do. I had failed a class for the first time in my life.

(As a professor, I must insert the thought that perhaps this was not the best way to deal with the due date for a paper, that Ms. Urash perhaps should have gone with her first idea without changing her thesis at such a late date, saving that new idea for some other time, some other course. So I do not exactly support the things Ms. Urash does here. But I am concerned here with the writing, which is crisp, descriptive, and powerful in how it creates before our eyes the scenes Ms. Urash is describing.)

Task 2.4

Now, revise the tale of your meeting based on what you have learned about Hemingway and his voice. Try to make it even more Hemingwayesque; have the characters talk like his characters; handle the dialogue and the description as he does. Bring the tale to an ending that might mimic the one in "A Day's Wait."

If you can do what Hemingway does—if you can become an accomplished "shower"—you will have an enormous power with the written word. You will be able to take someone who did not experience what you experienced—someone who missed the meeting, someone who lives on the other side of the world, someone who is not even born yet—and have him vicariously experience your life. That's astonishing, if you stop to think about it.

But there is more you might learn, different ways of rendering actions and scenes, and to do this, I want to introduce you to one of Hemingway's contemporaries, the Irish writer James Joyce. In his first collection of short stories, *Dubliners*, Joyce used a largely conventional descriptive style. But in his second work, a novel entitled *A Portrait of the Artist As a Young Man*, Joyce developed a strikingly different kind of narrative structure and narrative voice. By imitating this model, you can stretch your descriptive skills in new directions.

Task 2.5

Read the following selection from the beginning of *A Portrait of the Artist As a Young Man*. Read carefully, using your categories of macrostructure and microstructure to discover how this voice works.

Some background before you read:

James Joyce is one of the most influential writers of the twentieth century. Highly intellectual, creative, alternately political and fed up with politics, Joyce is part of that amazing flowering of writing that took place in Ireland in the first quarter of the century. His own attitude toward Ireland was vexed: he alternately loved and hated the place, and lived virtually his entire adult life in self-imposed exile. He described *Dubliners*, the collection of short stories mentioned above, as "a series of portraits of the sterility" of his homeland. Then, in *A Portrait of the Artist As a Young Man*, he created the story of a young man (who seems at times quite similar to Joyce himself) as he grows up in Dublin and rejects religion for Art. *Ulysses*, his masterpiece, takes Homer's *Odyssey* and fits it into one day—June 16, 1905—in the life of its hero, an ordinary Dubliner named Leopold Bloom. And his final work, *Finnegans Wake*, is a dream (or a nightmare, if you find it maddening); it begins in mid-sentence, ends with the first half of that sentence, and contains swatches and fragments in dozens of languages, all swirling in a "plot" that is full of hints and puns and leaps and is confusing as any dream. The following selection is the beginning of *Portrait*.

Once upon a time and a very good time it was there was a moocow coming down along the road and this moocow that was coming down along the road met a nicens little boy named baby tuckoo. . . .

His father told him that story: his father looked at him through a glass: he had a hairy face.

He was baby tuckoo. The moocow came down the road where Betty Byrne lived: she sold lemon platt.

> *O, the wild rose blossoms*
> *On the little green place.*

He sang that song. That was his song.

> *O, the green wothe botheth.*

When you wet the bed first it is warm then it gets cold. His mother put on the oilsheet. That had the queer smell.

His mother had a nicer smell than his father. She played on the piano the sailor's hornpipe for him to dance. He danced:

> *Tralala lala*
> *Tralala tralaladdy*
> *Tralala lala*
> *Tralala lala.*

Uncle Charles and Dante clapped. They were older than his father and mother but Uncle Charles was older than Dante.

Dante had two brushes in her press. The brush with the maroon velvet back was for Michael Davitt and the brush with the green velvet back was for Parnell. Dante gave him a cachou every time he brought her a piece of tissue paper.

The Vances lived in number seven. They had a different father and mother. They were Eileen's father and mother. When they were grown up he was going to marry Eileen. He hid under the table. His mother said:

—*O, Stephen will apologise.*

Dante said:

—*O, if not, the eagles will come and pull out his eyes.*

Pull out his eyes,
Apologise,
Apologise,
Pull out his eyes.

Apologise,
Pull out his eyes
Pull out his eyes,
Apologise.

The wide playgrounds were swarming with boys. All were shouting and the prefects urged them on with strong cries. The evening air was pale and chilly and after every charge and thud of the footballers the greasy leather orb flew like a heavy bird through the grey light. He kept on the fringe of his line, out of sight of his prefect, out of the reach of the rude feet, feigning to run now and then. He felt his body small and weak amid the throng of players and his eyes were weak and watery. Rody Kickham was not like that: he would be captain of the third line all the fellows said.

Rody Kickham was a decent fellow but Nasty Roche was

a stink. Rody Kickham had greaves in his number and a hamper in the refectory. Nasty Roche had big hands. He called the Friday pudding dog-in-the-blanket. And one day he had asked:

—What is your name?

Stephen had answered:

—Stephen Dedalus.

Then Nasty Roche had said:

—What kind of name is that?

And when Stephen had not been able to answer Nasty Roche had asked:

—What is your father?

Stephen had answered:

—A gentleman.

Then Nasty Roche had asked:

—Is he a magistrate?

He crept about from point to point on the fringe of his line, making little runs now and then. But his hands were bluish with cold. He kept his hands in the sidepockets of his belted grey suit. That was a belt round his pocket. And belt was also to give a fellow a belt. One day a fellow had said to Cantwell:

—I'd give you such a belt in a second.

Cantwell had answered:

—Go and fight your match. Give Cecil Thunder a belt. I'd like to see you. He'd give you a toe in the rump for yourself.

That was not a nice expression. His mother had told him not to speak with the rough boys in the college. Nice mother! The first day in the hall of the castle when she had said goodbye she had put up her veil double to her nose to kiss him: and her nose and eyes were red. But he had pretended not to see that she was going to cry. She was a nice mother but she was not so nice when she cried. And his father had given him two fiveshilling pieces for pocket money. And his father had told him if he wanted anything to write home to him and, whatever he did, never to peach on a fellow. Then at the door of the castle the rector had shaken hands with his father and mother, his soutane fluttering in the breeze, and the car had driven off with his father and mother on it. They had cried to him from car, waving their hands:

—Goodbye, Stephen, goodbye!

—Goodbye, Stephen, goodbye!

He was caught in the whirl of a scrimmage and, fearful of the flashing eyes and muddy boots, bent down to look through the legs. The fellows were struggling and groaning and their legs were rubbing and kicking and stamping. Then Jack Lawton's yellow boots dodged out the ball and all the other boots and legs ran after. He ran after them a little way and then stopped. It was useless to run on. Soon they would be going home for the holidays. After supper in the study hall he would change the number pasted up inside his desk from seventy-seven to seventy-six.[9]

If you have never encountered this type of writing before—which is called "stream of consciousness"—it can seem quite strange at first. But take your time and re-read, and you will begin to see what Joyce is doing: he describes not only the world "out there" which Hemingway tries to show us, but the inner river of thoughts that run through all of our minds in the midst of any day, any moment. (If you do not believe me, just try it. Sit quietly for a few minutes watching something, and pay attention to your thoughts. They will not stay focused on one thing for long.) Yet the leaps are not entirely random—they follow the associations, the associative leaps and turns, which lead us from one thought to the next. You might also notice how and when Joyce switches from "the world out there" to the "inner world" of consciousness, and back again.

Watch also the microstructures Joyce uses to convey the stream of consciousness. For one thing, he recognizes that we do not always think in complete sentences; we do not always use commas in our heads where "proper grammar" would have us do so. Sentences flow and bend and turn. At other times, our thoughts are short, compact.

Once you have read this carefully, and perhaps studied it with your partners, it is time to transform our minutes once again.

Task 2.6

Now, revise your minutes from Tasks 2.1 and 2.3 into Joyce's stream-of-consciousness style. To do this, close your eyes and place yourself in the meeting again. This time, describe not just what your senses recorded but also the thoughts that ran through your head as you sat at the meeting. Interweave the two by associative leaps as Joyce does.

❧

Bring your new "minutes"—by now they hardly look like minutes anymore, right?—to class. Share ideas with a partner or two, again looking for ways you can learn from one another to imitate Joyce more closely.

Earlier, you read Christi Urash's imitation of Hemingway. Now read how her imitation of Joyce transformed this into something different. Note how the events from her earlier narrative are still there, but now a new dimension occupies the description, emphasizing different things and creating a completely new look at the same event. If it helps, compare her two versions section by section.

> He wouldn't understand. She had to find him, but he wouldn't understand. Crazy things were always happening to Christi. How do you explain crazy things without sounding crazy? She knew he would roll his eyes. In his mind she knew he would be judging her, calling her lazy.
>
> She wished that she could be lazy. It would be nice to be on the Lazy River again. The sun warm on her face and the cool water pulling at her hair as she slowly drifted on her inner-tube. She loved water parks; water was always fun. She stepped in every puddle and walked barefoot in every stream she found. She hated those stupid amusement park rides her friends always wanted to go on over and over again. They were all nuts.
>
> Nuts are tasty, though. Little Debbie Nutty Butty Bars are great to take apart and eat in pieces. Andrea was Christi's

Nutty Buddy. They had been Nutty Buddies since fourth grade.

We all live in a yellow submarine,
a yellow submarine, a yellow submarine.

They always sang on the playground. She had never met anyone like Andrea and she really missed her. School was always so much fun with Andrea there. Christi was happy to be at the University though and she couldn't help smiling as she walked the campus grounds in search of him.

He used to be her favorite professor, but not anymore. She felt like he was laughing at her when she tried to tell him about her illness, as if he had heard better lies, but it was the truth. She had faced each of her teachers since the fourth grade with the same story and they had all been nicer than he was.

She found him walking to his car and she got his attention before he could get away. What was she going to say? She couldn't remember. She hadn't seen such a look since her mother had thought she was trying to get out of going to mass on a holy day of obligation. She didn't like being obligated to do anything as a teen. Her mother had just stood there with her weight shifted to one foot like a Hellenistic Greek statue in a *contraposto* stance. Her mom was a tiny little thing, just barely five feet tall, but she could scare the crap out of a grizzly bear with that look.

Fuzzy Wuzzy was a bear,
Fuzzy Wuzzy had no hair.

Fuzzy Wuzzy didn't believe Christi's story. He told her to have her paper ready at the beginning of class the next day. She spent the rest of that night in her cramped apartment working on the paper. She had thought writing about her pirate ancestor, Francis Drake, would be a breeze. Instead, he pillaged her brain, ransacked her nerves, and left her feeling as ruined as the cities he had burned.

She had watched a house burn before. It was terrifying and beautiful. The smell of the burning wood reminded her of cold winter nights in Salt Lake, sitting in front of her friend Liz's fireplace. Fire was fascinating. At the end of every school year, Christi and her brothers would light a fire in the barbecue. They would sacrifice their notebooks and homework to the hungry orange monster.

Christi worked through the night. Half an hour before class she was almost finished. She was very proud of herself. The paper was actually pretty good. Bang! What was that? The computer screen was black. Disbelief, shock and fear swirled around her. No! No! No! It's time for a heart attack. If she could just go to the emergency room she might pass the class. Maybe the power would come back and the paper would miraculously be there. Had she saved her work?

No! Damn it! She couldn't believe it. She called the apartment office and the electric company. It was a breaker outside, just her building. She was out of time and out of ideas. In her head like a broken record she repeated, "No! No way. Damn it, no! Oh, God, no! No way..." All her work had been sucked down the drain. The semester was sucked down the drain. If she lost her scholarship, years of work would be sucked down that grimy hole where all wasted time swirled away.

> *Toilet paper go down the hole.*
> *Ducky go down the hole.*

Tiny Toons was on everyday after school when Christi was young. Baby Ducky was really funny. His favorite thing to do was flush objects down the toilet. The scene usually ended when he flushed himself down the hole.

> *Ducky go down the hole.*
> *Sir Francis go down the hole.*
> *Christi go down the hole.*

Ms. Urash is a bright, thoughtful young woman, but at this point was not always confident of her writing skills. She had entered the course with no knowledge of James Joyce, and with no experience of writing in this style. Yet through her close reading and close imitation of Joyce, she expanded her horizons, her set of writing skills, in this direction, and gave herself some tools to relate to others—to you and me, who were not there—this stressful day in her life. Try to learn what you can from her work—which is, I must be quick to admit, not perfect, either. Explore ways you can improve your own Joyce imitation by reading her attempt.

Great Ideas: Realism Revisited; Language and Its Limitations

Students often find stream-of-consciousness writing strange, different, odd. But is it really so? In chapter 1, I discussed how Impressionism had transformed art, and transformed the art of description. Realism can't simply be what is "out there," the Impressionists maintained: it must be a record of the impressions that come to our senses, not the reality our brain puts together and understands from these sensations. Joyce's stream-of-consciousness pushes those ideas a step further. If Impressionism asks what is "realism," Joyce wonders whether impressions themselves are not enough to be truly "realistic." For do we only receive impressions from outside? Don't those impressions collide with what is running around in our thoughts, ideas, reflections? That is, if one were to produce a "realistic" account of "what really happened" at a meeting, shouldn't it include all of the things that were running through Christi Urash's head, including comments on people, snatches of songs, and more? Taken from this viewpoint, all of the innovations in writing are not attempts to be "different" or "odd," but attempts to capture even more of reality.

The other question here might be: *can* language capture reality? Can there ever be "realism" in any complete way? Is language inherently flawed, unable to truthfully reflect reality? You might see that Hemingway and Joyce approached this question differently. But each is, in his own way, suspicious of language. Hemingway appears worried that too much language—too many flowery phrases, too many similes, metaphors, symbols, and so forth—gets in the way, falsifying reality. So he strips down his language, saying as little as possible, trying to be as direct as possible. Joyce occupies the other end of the spectrum: he tries to throw as much language as he can at reality, using every resource of language (and even inventing a few new ones), as if, as one of my teachers, Professor Alan Howard, has said, he needs a huge net to throw over reality, to gather in as much as he can. (In *Finnegans Wake* he stretches it well beyond what you see here, using different languages and even root-words from long-dead languages like Sanskrit to try to make his net even bigger and wider.) But this very conception betrays his fear that some of reality always escapes his net.

You might consider where you find yourself in this debate. Do you tend to believe that we should be "short and sweet" in our language, "clear and concise," avoiding as much floweriness and artistry as possible? Or do you believe we should do the opposite, using all of the resources of image, symbol, metaphor, floweriness, innovation? Answering this question is a way of getting at your ideas about language and exploring your own core voices.[10]

Task 2.7

Now, revise your Joyce imitation, picking up more features of his voice, both macro- and micro-. Have a spirit of experimentation here; after all, Joyce was at the time experimenting with something no one had attempted before.

Finally, it is important to think about what you have done here, what you have learned, what you have accomplished—as well as what is still strange and confusing and difficult. Take some time. Read others' attempts in this chapter. Share your work with classmates. Then move on to the final assignment.

Task 2.8

Reflect for a page or two on what you have learned from this assignment. What have you learned about describing actions? In what ways has this improved your writing? In what situations might you wish to use these skills? Which voice do you find closest to your own voice—the "minutes" voice? Hemingway's? Joyce's? Or someone completely different? How did imitating the others bring out the distinctive sound of your own voice?

Why We're Doing This

It seems like it should be easy to tell someone "what happened." But again, it is not as easy as it might at first appear. So this is a crucial skill, giving you a great deal of power with your words. Mastering this skill is crucial in improving your writing. "Showing" takes time, and learning how to do it takes practice. Yet, like the description you learned in chapter 1, it goes beyond a simple writing skill; it teaches patient attention to your world, for to describe accurately, you must "caress the details" of your world, noticing the things that are significant, that make meaning, that convey that meaning to others, whether that is a gesture, a way of sitting, a curve in someone's lips. Furthermore, it trains you in the skill of artistic selection: you have to decide, and then emphasize, the details that make a difference, that will contribute to the meanings you wish to convey. There is more than one way to describe (even more ways than I have shown you here). By imitating two of the great masters of description, you should be gaining these skills and learning how it is done. And along the way, you have apprenticed yourself to two of the great writers of the twentieth century, which is no small thing for a few days' work.

Extra Exercises for Those Who Want to Do More[11]

Practice, practice, practice your description skills, your ability to "show." Just do this anytime, anywhere. Whenever you have a minute or two—sitting in a coffee shop, watching your family watch TV—take out a piece of paper and begin "showing" what you see, hear, smell, touch. Use memories, drawing a sketch that can bring alive for someone events that happened a year ago, ten years ago, yesterday. The more you do this, the better your observation skills will get, and the better your descriptive skills will get.

Take a passage from a favorite author, or some famous author—and "translate" it into another author's style. Take any two writers you like—it helps if their voices are completely different. How would William Faulkner describe a scene in a Jane Austen novel? Then take a scene in a Faulkner novel and put it in Jane Austen's voice. How would Toni Morrison describe a scene from The Scarlet Letter? *It can be fascinating to see how the style and structure completely change the way the scene comes across. The very subject matter changes.*

Do the same thing with authors whose styles might at first appear to be similar rather than radically different. Virginia Woolf, James Joyce, and William Faulkner all employ a version of the stream-of-consciousness style, yet one could hardly be mistaken for either of the other two. Take a single passage and translate it into the different styles of the other authors. Then take three writers who use a terse, restrained style, as Hemingway does. As you search for the small differences and try to imitate them, you will improve your writing—and your critical reading skills—even more.

Read, read, read. I simply cannot emphasize enough that good writing comes from long, deep immersion in the words of great writers. Read intensely in one writer until you begin to know that writer's characteristic style, gestures, voice. And read widely in very different sorts of writers, so you begin to stretch your stock of voices in different ways.

Chapter Three

Voices of Definition:
Making Complex Distinctions

A fter your work with description, turning to a chapter on definition may seem a dull and bloodless thing. But I want to encourage you to think otherwise. Definitions are not simple affairs; they require careful distinctions and precise thinking, a flexible mind, and an ability to see complex entities clearly. If you can define terms accurately, you can see through to the core of what you are discussing, and can direct the discussion towards this truth. Conversely, if you do not define well and accurately, you can find yourself mired in confusion and miss essential points further along in your investigation. Read Plato's dialogues, and see how often Socrates is concerned with defining terms carefully as the crucial step to establishing the truth of what we know.

So definition is important in your own attempt to discover the truth about a thing, a concept, a situation. Definition is also important rhetorically, that is, in your attempts to persuade someone else of the truth. For instance, it is almost a cliché that the abortion debate in the United States comes down to a difference in definition: is the fetus already, from conception (or at some other point in gestation), a *human being*? To what extent? Or is it a not-quite-human *fetus*, only potentially a human being? What is a human being, anyway? If it is a human being, does that predication "human being" entitle it to the same rights as humans living outside the womb? If it is not yet a human being, does it have any rights at all? That is, how does one *define* this thing—this assembly of cells, this six-week-old something with a tail, this three-month-old something with a beating heart, limbs, and many functioning systems? These are not simple, or unimportant, matters: political forces, enormous sums of government funding, and yes, lives and their meaning rest on one's definitions of these key terms.

Here is another, more mundane example. In Georgia in 2001, a controversy erupted over whether cheerleading should be considered a sport. Supporters of this claim argued that modern cheerleaders no longer merely stand around, shake pom-pons, and try to get the crowd to yell; they perform difficult gymnastic routines requiring enormous strength, agility, and stamina. But is it a *sport*? Does not a sport involve some kind of athletic *competition*? Well, cheerleaders do compete—they attend competitions and pit themselves against other squads. But is this competition *essential* to being a cheerleader, as competition is essential to the sport of basketball, or is it an ancillary activity? After all, marching bands attend competitions, too, but competition is not essential to making music. Perhaps cheerleading's essential activity is to lead cheers, and the competition is only something squads do on the side, interested as they might be from time to time in which squad does it best.

Definitions, therefore, try to get at the essence of a thing, an activity.

But actually, there was more to this issue, a lurking political, financial, and thus rhetorical question that it took a second glance to see. Because the federal mandate known as Title IX requires schools to offer equal sports programs for men and women, many schools have been scrambling to add women's sports in order to come into compliance with this federal mandate. Some schools have even cut men's sports to achieve this equality rather than add more women's sports. So defining cheerleading as a "sport" would allow these schools to count these (largely female) cheerleaders in their numbers of women athletes, and thereby not add more women's sports or cut any men's sports.

So definitions are important, one of those foundational skills for all good writing, for all good thinking, for all good and true rhetoric. If we are going to learn the basic, apprentice skills of writing, this is one of those crucial things to learn, to practice, like a painter's apprentice learning to mix paints, or the jazz musician learning his scales and chords. But again, you will not learn just by thinking about definitions in the abstract; you will learn by apprenticing yourself to great writers who make definition a key moment in their writing. In this chapter let us continue our process of apprenticeship, then, by learning from one of the great extended definitions in all of literature: Paul's definition of love in his letter to the Corinthians during the earliest years of the Christian era. We will then experiment with a marvelous definition from a woman with almost no formal education, Sojourner Truth. These are truly masterful definitions, willing to take on two of the slipperiest subjects known to humans and succeeding, in most readers' estimations, marvelously.

But as always, we begin first with a warm-up exercise designed to practice your invention skills and give you some material with which to work during this chapter's exercises.

Task 3.1

Brainstorm, free-write, and use other discovery methods to find a subject you wish to define. Try to think of a subject sufficiently complex and various that it will require some serious effort on your part—that is, you might not wish to define "dog" but something more fascinating and involved—perhaps something abstract, or an emotion, or an attitude. Once you have your subject, rough out a working and workable definition, knowing that this will be a rough draft. (Or if you choose "dog," you might think in creative ways about playing with that idea.)

Bring your definition back to class, and as always, read it aloud to two classmates. Compare what you wrote with their attempts. Did you capture the essence of the thing, or did your partners find things you may have left out, or aspects that you did not consider? Make some notes about how to improve your definition.[1]

Task 3.2

Read, slowly and carefully, Paul's definition of love below. You may have heard or read this passage before, but even if you have, this time read it as if for the first time. That is, look at it with fresh eyes as a writer trying to define a complex subject. What sort of definitional techniques does he use? What does he do to frame the definition and then zero in on the essential aspects? Take some notes as you read about how his definition differs from the one you wrote in Task 3.1.

Some background before you read:

Paul of Tarsus is, after Jesus of Nazareth himself, one of the most important figures in the history of Christianity. In his early life he was a Jew named Saul, well educated in both the traditions of Judaic thought and Hellenistic (Greek) philosophy, and he tells us he persecuted the new movement of Christianity as it grew, arresting and imprisoning its followers; he was present, Luke tells in the Acts of the Apostles, at the stoning of Stephen, traditionally the first Christian martyr. Sometime later he had a famous conversion experience in which God came to him in a blinding light and said, "Saul, Saul, why are you persecuting me?" Afterwards he changed his name to Paul and became one of the greatest evangelists for the new movement, traveling throughout Asia Minor; eventually he was sent to Rome, the capital of the known world, where tradition tells us he was martyred there, beheaded at the time of the Emperor Nero.

The following excerpt is taken from the First Letter to the Corinthians. Paul had visited Corinth (in Greece)—a city known for its wild ways and strong pagan cult of Aphrodite that included religious prostitution—about the year 50 A.D., and had established a Christian community there. Now, some five or six years later, he has received unhappy news from the city: factions have broken out among the Christian groups there, pagan practices were reintroduced among the community, and a member was openly living in an incestuous relationship. Christianity itself was being interpreted, by a minority in the community, as a kind of special wisdom for the few rather than a message of grace for all, and some were elevating the idea of ecstatic prayer and special spiritual messages over the importance of charitable works. Most scholars believe the majority of the community was not so disordered, but Paul clearly writes in a concerned tone about what has become of the group he founded. Here, in perhaps the most famous passage of all his writings—a passage often read at weddings—Paul defines (and hymns) what many have thought to be the core of Christianity: love. But he carefully defines what he means by love as the core of his message to the community he left behind; he means it to be a wake-up call and a ringing summons back to the message he originally preached to them. Watch how a careful definition helps Paul achieve his purpose.

You will read here the King James Version (KJV), a translation produced in the early seventeenth century—during Shakespeare's lifetime—by a committee of scholars commissioned by King James I of England. Though modern scholars fault it at times for inaccuracies, it has for many years been the version of the Bible that has influenced writers of all sorts for its sonority and rhythms, its Latinate phrasings and beautiful use of the language. (I have a friend, a classicist and theologian, who is quite sure that God speaks ecclesiastical Latin, but I have it on good authority that the Almighty, when He deigns to use human language, speaks KJV English.) This version uses the word "charity"—the most direct translation of the Latin *caritas*—whereas other versions use the word "love."[2]

[1]Though I speak with the tongues of men and of angels, and have not charity, I am become as sounding brass, or a tinkling cymbal.

[2]And though I have the gift of prophecy, and understand all mysteries, and all knowledge: and though I have all faith, so that I could remove mountains, and have not charity, I am nothing.

[3]And though I bestow all my good to feed the poor, and though I give my body to be burned, and have not charity, it profiteth me nothing.

⁴Charity suffereth long, and is kind; charity envieth not: charity vaunteth not itself, is not puffed up;

⁵Doth not behave itself unseemly, seeketh not her own, is not easily provoked, thinketh no evil;

⁶Rejoiceth not in iniquity, but rejoiceth in the truth;

⁷Beareth all things, believeth in all things, hopeth all things, endureth all things.

⁸Charity never faileth: but whether there be prophecies, they shall fail; whether there be tongues, they shall cease; whether there be knowledge, it shall vanish away.

⁹For we know in part, and we prophesy in part.

¹⁰But when that which is perfect is come, then that which is in part shall be done away.

¹¹When I was a child, I spake as a child, I understood as a child, I thought as a child: but when I became a man, I put away childish things.

¹²For now we see through a glass, darkly; but then face to face: now I know in part; but then shall I know even as also I am known.

¹³And now abideth faith, hope, charity, these three; but the greatest of these is charity.³

Task 3.3

Now, take your definition from Task 3.1 and rewrite it, imitating the style and structure of Paul's definition. Try to imitate the style of Paul's work, from the overarching structure of definition and elaboration, to some of the unusual phrasing, to the comparisons through simile and metaphor. Look at individual sentences and try to imitate their structure and vocabulary.

To complete this assignment, you will have to go back and re-read the biblical passage very carefully as you write. You'll have to look at the large and small ways that this "voice" is created.

Look at the macrostructure of Paul's style; that is, notice the large blocks of structure that set up this voice. Look further: which of the kinds of definitions given on pages

55 to 57 does Paul use? How does he deploy them at different times? Why do you think he does this?

Look at the microstructure of Paul's style. What little turns of phrase make this voice sound as it does? What sort of diction (that is, word choice or vocabulary) makes this sound so different? Are the sentences long and ornate, or are they short and concise? Are they full of similes and images and metaphors, or are they straightforward and flat? Does the writing refer to or allude to other writings? What other little things make up the sound of this voice? Try to do what those things do.

When you are done writing, bring your definition to class. Share it with two classmates. Read each other's imitations. Now, compare your rules to the original King James version. What different features did your classmates notice and imitate in the original? How did your definition change from the earliest draft version in your own voice to this version in the King James voice? Did putting the definition in this voice add clarity or create more ambiguity? What should be done about that? What else can you learn from your partners' definitions that you will want to include in your work? Make some notes for when you revise your rules.[4]

Here is a student, Diana Fernandez, who has imitated Paul's definition of charity. If you know Portia's speech on mercy from Shakespeare's *The Merchant of Venice*, you might find interesting connections here. Watch how she closely imitates the syntax, rhythm, and diction of the King James model.

[1]Though I walk with power and authority, and have not mercy, I am become as a ceaseless wave of the destructive sea.

[2]And though I have the gift of truth, and suffocate all false promises, and all misleading: and though I have all talents, so that I could exceed the great works of art, and have not mercy, I am nothing.

[3]And though I bestow all my justice to uphold order, give to all what they are due, and have not mercy, it profits me nothing.

⁴Mercy is grace, and is a gift; it is not expected: mercy is not required, is not deserved;

⁵Does not grow from weakness, act without purpose, is not lightly granted, stems from strength;

⁶Rejoices not in failing, but rejoices in triumph;

⁷Mercy never fails: but where there are powers, they shall fail; where there are talents, they shall expire; where there is justice, it shall be inept.

⁸For we are imperfectly truthful, and we are imperfectly just.

⁹But when perfection is come, then all imperfection shall be undone.

Task 3.4

Now revise your definition, trying to craft it even closer to the King James model, trying to make your own voice sound more "biblical." You will probably have to read the text at least one more time as you write, poring over it carefully for features to imitate. Bring it to class and share this version with your classmates.

When you are done, work with fellow students, seeing what you changed, what you retained, and what you can still learn. Go back over the original model, studying which features you considered most important to the voice and which ones you decided to omit or vary. Were you able to define the subject clearly and completely? Were you able to evoke the full nature of the topic? How did your voice shift as you worked on the imitation?

Great Ideas: Different Types of Definition and the Nature of Poetry

When you think of defining, you probably think first of the dictionary and the types of definition you find there, but there are really several types of definition, and it is worth thinking about and practicing them. The dictionary kind of definition is a *stipulative definition*, which tries to achieve, as precisely as possible, the finite limits of the term under consideration. It has two parts: the genus, and the species, or difference:

Man is a rational animal.

A lasagna is a baked pasta dish with layered flat noodles separated by cheese and other fillings.

Such a definition starts by setting up the genus, the general group to which the item belongs (an animal, a dish), then begins to specify it, or differentiate from other items in this generic group, first by saying it is a pasta dish, and then even more so by saying it has flat noodles and layers of fillings and is baked. The method here is like branching down a tree, getting more and more specific until one reaches the narrow branch on which fits only the item you are describing. If a stipulative definition works—that is, if it has accurately defined—one has moved from the general to the one specific item where no other items fit: no other item matches the stipulations you have placed upon this generic group. Thus as you are writing a stipulative definition, you must be very careful first to name the general category to which it belongs (an automobile is a vehicle of transport, not a piece of jewelry) and then specify it carefully so that you distinguish it from all other items in this general group (differentiating an automobile from an airplane, a boat, and even a truck).

But there are other kinds of definition as well. One is the *definition by example*, where you do not precisely stipulate the item, but point to something so that your audience will grasp it quickly:

Dialect is when you say "skillet" and I say "frying pan."

Philosophers are people such as Plato and Aristotle.

You can quickly see the difficulties of definition by example: it does not give the precision of the stipulative definition, and your audience may not grasp the concept very clearly, especially if, for instance in the second example, they have no experience with the examples, with Plato or Aristotle. But it does give a concreteness that often helps others come to some understanding of the term in question. Defining "pun" as "a humorous use of a word or words with two or more meanings; play on words," as my *Oxford Desk Dictionary: American Edition* does, may be terribly abstract and abstruse, and it may not help someone as much as a quick example of a pun. Often, therefore, combining stipulative definitions and definitions by example can be very powerful. Many dictionaries will give examples of the terms they define for this very reason.

An interesting form is the *definition by analogy*, wherein you suggest what something is by comparing it to something else:

Odysseus' oikos is like an extended family.

Dante's hell is an inverted cone.

In this kind of definition, you do not specify as carefully as you do in a stipulative definition, and in that sense, you risk something: you are again not narrowing down the item to one precise thing. Yet you gain something as well: perhaps a sense of the whole of the thing, its contours and qualities. And as long as you know that a definition by analogy is not as precise—as long as you do not mistake your analogical definitions for stipulative ones—you can learn a great deal by this method. When I am dealing with especially complex subjects, I often will try to construct an analogy for myself: "Ancient Rome was like [twenty-first-century America, or the British Empire, or Anglo-Saxon England]"; "the spirit of Greek philosophy was . . . ." Now, by testing how well my analogy fits—and equally importantly, by how it does not fit, for every analogy is both a likeness and a difference—I can learn a great deal about my subject. Once I think of an ancient Greek *oikos* (the large political unit that made up "Ithaka" or "Mycenae" in the archaic Greek world) like an extended family, I must also ask myself how it was *not* like one, and in so doing, I come to a more precise understanding of this fascinating topic that is the core of Homer's *Odyssey*.

One might even say that poetry is this form of definition writ large, for what does a poet (here I mean poet in the largest sense, a *maker*, including novelists, playwrights, etc.) do but create analogies? And not just locally in their similes and metaphors, though they clearly do this. No, poets by their very nature create fictional worlds, analogies to our real world—the Bath of Jane Austen, the Purgatory of Dante, the Scotland of Shakespeare's *Macbeth*. A poet by his very nature says, "Life is like this," and asks us to compare that world to our own world, to see how these fictional worlds fit our experience of, well, reality, life. And how they don't fit—the great poets are always keenly aware of the fictionality of their fictions, as Shakespeare is in *The Tempest*. Poetry, then, asks us to learn from these analogies, these definitions by comparison.

Task 3.5

Read Sojourner Truth's famous oration "And Ain't I a Woman?" below. You will notice that it, too, is based on an implicit act of definition. Read carefully how Truth constructs her speech to answer the charges against women, developing an understanding of women and the human throughout.

Some background before you read:

Sojourner Truth was born into slavery in New York in 1795; she gained her freedom in 1827 and soon became known for traveling the country and delivering fiery abolitionist sermons. She met Harriet Beecher Stowe, author of *Uncle Tom's Cabin*, and many of the important preachers and ministers of her day. Tall and dark, with a powerful voice, she made an imposing figure upon which many commented. The following speech, delivered extemporaneously, was made at a women's rights convention in Akron, Ohio, in 1851. Frances Gage, a feminist leader who had helped organize the conference and was presiding, wrote an account of what happened. Several well-known ministers came to the meeting on its second day, attacking the meeting and its cause. One spoke on the "superior intellect" of men; another lectured on the "manhood of Christ," suggesting that if Jesus had wanted to show women equal he would have given some sign of it. A third spoke on the sin of the first woman, Eve. Sneers began to break out from men and older boys who were looking on from the balcony.

At this point Sojourner Truth, almost six feet tall, rose from her seat in the corner. Many of the women in the meeting had feared this, and they implored Ms. Gage not to let her speak, fearing that the women's rights cause would become entangled with the even more hot-button questions of slavery and abolition. But Gage allowed her to speak, and Gage reproduced her speech in this way:

"Wall, chilern, whar dar is so much racket dar must be somethin' out o' kilter. I tink dat 'twixt de niggers[6] of de Souf and de womin at de Norf, all talkin' 'bout rights, de white men will be in a fix pretty soon. But what's all dis here talkin' 'bout?

Dat man ober dar say dat womin needs to be helped into carriages, and lifted ober ditches, and to hab de best place everywhar. Nobody eber helps me into carriages, or ober mud-puddles, or gibs me any best place!" And raising herself to her full height, and her voice to a pitch like rolling thunder, she asked, "And a'n't I a woman? Look at me! Look at my arm! (and she bared her right arm to the shoulder, showing her tremendous muscular power). I have ploughed, and planted, and gathered into barns, and no man could head me! And a'n't I a woman? I could work as much and eat as much as a man—when I could get it—and bear de lash as well! And a'n't I a woman? I have borne thirteen chilern, and seen 'em mos' all sold off to slavery, and when I cried out with my mother's grief, none but Jesus heard me! And a'n't I a woman?[7]

"Den dey talks 'bout dis ting in de head; what dis dey call it?" ("Intellect," whispered some one near.) "Dat's it, honey. What's dat got to do wid womin's rights or nigger's rights? If my cup won't hold but a pint, and yourn holds a quart, wouldn't ye be mean not to let me have my little half-measure full?" And she pointed her significant finger, and sent a keen glance at the minister who had made the argument. The cheering was long and loud.

"Den dat little man in black dar, he say women can't have as much rights as men, 'cause Christ wan't a woman! Whar did your Christ come from?" Rolling thunder couldn't have stilled that crowd, as did those deep, wonderful tones, as she stood there with outstretched arms and eyes of fire. Raising her voice still louder, she repeated, "Whar did your Christ come from? From God and a woman! Man had nothin' to do wid Him." Oh, what a rebuke that was to that little man.

Turning again to another objector, she took up the defense of Mother Eve. I can not follow her through it all. It was pointed, and witty, and solemn; eliciting at almost every sentence deafening applause; and she ended by asserting: "If de fust woman God ever made was strong enough to turn de world upside down all alone, dese women togedder (and she glanced her eye over the platform) ought to be able to turn it back, and get it right side up again! And now dey is asking to do it, de men better let 'em." Long-continued cheering greeted this. "'Bleeged to ye for hearin' on me, and now ole Sojourner han't got nothin' more to say."

You will again need to read closely and carefully to see the subtle ways this speech works upon its listeners, how Truth moves to make her points, how she defines "woman" through her speech, how her turns of phrase appeal to her audience.

Task 3.6

Now revise your earlier definition so that it imitates Sojourner Truth's voice, style, and structure. You may need to add or delete some aspects of your definition. Try to capture the energy and urgency of her speech in your new definitional piece.

☙

You may want to explore the voice of this piece in more detail. How is it that such writing (or speaking) "works" so well when, by the standards of grammar handbooks, it uses the English language so poorly? How are we to account for effective writing that breaks "the rules" so flagrantly? Or *does* Truth's language, except for its dialectal differences, break these rules? That is, which are the *crucial* rules of effective writing and which are *peripheral*? As you begin to improve your own writing and deepen your own understanding of these abilities, you surely will want to confront the differences between the crucial aspects of good writing and the surface attraction of "correctness."

Ashley Wood has adapted and imitated Sojourner Truth's definitional strategy in the following essay on "beauty." She does not try to capture the dialectal power of Truth's language, but she does aim for her negative definitions and her ironic sense of her subject.

From recent television programs and magazine articles, I gather there is much to be said today concerning the topic of beauty, most of it falling under the umbrella of *healthy living*: a nobler venture, certainly, than the pursuit of external excellence. But I wonder what it is we are talking about. One would think, with all of the information we are privy to regarding beauty, and with so many exciting developments in the technological realm of self-improvement, we would all have achieved excellence by now, and yet we still fall short, always short of perfection.

Vogue tells me that if I highlight my cheeks in a certain manner, and sweep a certain shadow over my eyelid I will be beautiful. If I flatter my figure with a certain cut of trouser and my skin tone with a certain shade of blue, and if I use a certain cream to moisturize away my wrinkles and a certain concealer to hide the dark circles under my eyes, I will be nearer to perfection. But I have done this, and still I am not beautiful.

Shape Magazine tells me I must complete four to five one-hour sessions of cardiovascular exercise per week, supplemented with two to three weekly weight-training sessions to achieve optimum *health*, for that is the number dictated by my body type. I must drink only water bottled at a certain spring, avoid carbohydrates that are not complex, and consume only organic produce. I must refrain from foods containing refined sugar, white flour, enriched flour or bleached flour, wheat, dairy, trans fats, saturated fats, processed ingredients, additives or preservatives, caffeine, and artificial sweeteners. Only then, they tell me, will my body be beautiful. But I have done this; I have hired a personal trainer and put in hour upon hour at a private gym, and I have followed a special diet specifically designed for me by a nutritionist, and still—I am not beautiful.

And the television tells me I must drive a certain car, wear a certain designer, carry a certain bag, tote a certain tiny animal, buy a certain house in a certain zip code, gain membership to a certain exclusive club, attend certain parties, befriend certain musicians, donate to certain charities, be seen at certain restaurants and benefits, take certain vacations (where I must stay in certain suites), cheer for certain sports teams, perform a certain mixture of yoga and pilates, and date certain men who either make or stand to inherit large fortunes. I have tried to do these things: I have tried, stretching my physical and mental limitations to their utmost and exhausting my resources, financial and otherwise, and still, I am not beautiful.

Moreover, my television requires that I surgically smooth the flaws in my appearance, while surgically enhancing my natural attributes. It informs me I must avoid the sun and certain types of air, and once my skin has attained the appropriate level of suppleness I must reveal as much of it as possible, at all times.

Above all, I must not smoke.

And I have tried, but what more can I do? I, who have cellulite, and spider veins, and crow's feet, and sun damage—I, who have whitening hair and yellowing teeth and stretch marks and scars and collapsed ankles? I—overweight and undernourished?

Maybe it is not so terrible. My mother is not beautiful, nor her mother before her. Perhaps it is better to leave beauty to those more willing than I to procure it.

Task 3.7

Write for a while in your journal about this experience.[8] How did imitating Paul's work make you consider your topic more carefully—and think more fully about what it means and how to define it? How did shifting into this voice restrict you, and how did it free you to do more? How did then shifting into Sojourner Truth's voice restrict, free, or shape you? How will this make you more sensitive to the rhetorical power of definition and its usefulness in your writing? What else did you learn from this exercise?

Why We're Doing This

As I mentioned in the introduction to this chapter, definition is such a crucial skill in discovering the truth about the world, and in relating that truth to others, that I have devoted a full chapter to it. If you can define the terms you use more precisely, if you can begin to see how your definitions work and use those workings more thoughtfully, if you can look at the ways others define their terms—explicitly and implicitly—then you will gain a great deal of control over your own thoughts, be able to convey your thoughts more effectively to others, and be able to analyze others' definitions, thoughts, and arguments with more skill and power. Definition simply is one of the foundations for both logic (the art of discovering truth) and rhetoric (the art of persuading others of the truth as you have discovered it). So be sure you have mastered this skill, and return to it often as you continue to improve your writing.

Extra Exercises for Those Who Want to Do More

Find an editorial or column in a newspaper or magazine. Carefully note all the places where the author explicitly defines terms, and note which kinds of definitions he or she uses. Analyze them—are they accurate definitions? Then look for places where terms are defined implicitly, and analyze those. Why does the author define some terms explicitly and leave others implicit? What types of definitions does the author use, where, and why?

Find other essays that are largely devoted to defining a key term or terms. What is the point of the entire essay? That is, why go to the effort of defining this term so carefully? Try imitating this essay and building your own definition using its structure and style.

If you have never done so, you might visit a predominantly African-American church where call-and-response is used in the services. Note how the method works rhetorically, then explore the fundamental ways call-and-response informs music (especially jazz, blues, rock, and rap) and other art forms born out of the African-American experience. How does this method "define" the important concepts in the sermon or the piece?

Chapter Four

Voices of Authority: Making Rules

*I*n the last chapter, you explored how to write clear and helpful definitions, how to lead someone to see what makes a thing what it is and not something else. Writing definitions is, as I explored, a matter of thinking through the reality of a thing—what it is like, and what it is not like; what makes it part of a group, and what distinguishes it from other members of that group.

Making rules for a group requires much more than that sense of what a thing. For one thing, it requires the imagination to think ahead and consider: what might happen? What do we want to have happen? Here you imagine not a thing, but a group of people; here you must anticipate in advance behaviors and problems and deal with them. Centrally, however, you must create rules that will help ensure a community with united purposes and similar actions, and envision what will happen when someone violates the community's expected norms. Thus, writing rules is about standards and consequences. Like definitions, writing rules requires precision, a careful choice of words, and control over the ambiguity and variety of meanings those words can create.

Of course, most rules do not result from a prior act of imagination; they are hammered out over time. A group—let's say, a chess club or a sorority—operates for a while, then decides it would be helpful to lay out its already-agreed-upon standards for behavior. Later, when someone does something the group finds unacceptable, it reconvenes and establishes a rule outlawing that behavior in the future. Rules thus tend to grow and change over time out of the experience of the community. Still, in these cases the skills of verbal precision and imagining future events and consequences are important and worth learning. Therefore, our next stage in writing consists of exploring how we can use words to set limits, describe situations, and importantly, create a voice that gives us authority.

That word *authority* is significant here. For not just anyone gets to make rules. Or one could say: anyone can make up rules, but they will only be listened to if they come from a voice with authority. Or I could say it a different way: the amount of authority changes how one gets to speak. At least in my house, my parents were the ones with real authority. Mom was able to say, "Take off your shoes! Don't track that mud in the house." My sister couldn't say that to me; I would just stick out my tongue and saunter off. When your boss is yelling at you, you do not often get to say, "Boss, lower your voice. That is no tone in which to address a fellow adult." You have to put it differently—right?—because you do not have authority. (Either that, or you can just say, "Take this job and . . ."—well, you know the rest.) And the boss, also, had better find a more thoughtful and useful way to display his authority, or most of his employees will move on to happier and more encouraging working conditions. Authority therefore is complex; its sources reside sometimes in social, political, and economic status, but ultimately, and most deeply, in truth and justice; Adolf Hitler had enormous power, but he did not rule with authority.[1]

Among people who are otherwise equals, those with more knowledge and experience are generally granted authority. Though many people like to share their opinions about sports, a professional coach with decades of experience and several championships can speak with more authority than the guy watching the game in a bar. In a question about Brahms's piano concertos, you would listen to the opinions of a pianist who has played Carnegie Hall before you would listen to me, an English professor who took a year of piano in fifth grade, would you not?

That is, you would trust him to be more *authoritative*, to speak with more truth and assuredness, on this subject—that is, until he perhaps showed through his language and arguments that he only played ragtime and jazz piano and had very little experience with Brahms's music. Mother Teresa of Calcutta was a simple woman with no Ph.D. and assuredly little political power, yet when she spoke, people—even those initially hostile—listened to her. She spoke with authority, the authority gained from having lived a life with integrity and charity.

In this chapter, we will together confront one of the most important and authoritative texts in Western, and indeed world, culture—the Ten Commandments—and we confront them in one of the most important, influential, and authoritative voices in English writing: the voice of the King James Bible. (You may know the Ten Commandments by heart, and if so, that is wonderful; in my experience, however, some people think they know them but are surprised when they read the actual text.) This set of rules has been one of the most important and far-reaching in all of world culture. Few would deny its importance historically, and many still live by them (or at least struggle daily to do so). This particular version is important for another reason: the "King James" version of the Bible has exerted an incalculable influence on writing in English, from poets to novelists to essayists. As I noted in the last chapter, this translation was commissioned by King James I during a time of religious controversy, when England swung between a possibly pro-Roman Catholic Anglican hierarchy and radically Protestant groups. It was meant to unite the English in their "Middle Way" between these two extremes. It was not the first translation of the Bible into English, but because of its authority (it was produced by a group of the best scholars of its day—one joke is that it is the only decent piece of writing ever produced by a committee), its startling rhythmic beauty, and its existence during a time when English was experiencing an enormously powerful period (this was, after all, during the lives of Shakespeare, Ben Jonson, John Donne, and John Milton), the King James Version remains for many the most compelling translation of the Bible into English. Poets even today write that its images and rhythms sound in their heads from years of exposure to it, and that its language has shaped their own sense of what English sounds like at its best. What can be better, then, as we imitate our way to better writing than to get into our heads the sound of this book?

But first, a warm-up exercise to find your subject and begin exploring voice.

Task 4.1

Find the written rules of some organization. It might be a club, a sorority, a team, or some other organization. If you cannot find any, try writing up the rules for an organization yourself. Try to cover all of the important situations and problems that might arise, and provide for punishments when the rules are broken.[2]

Bring the rules to class. Trade with a classmate, and read them aloud. On whose authority are these rules made? How does the writing attempt to claim the authority to make these rules? How does the writing attempt to cover possible situations? That is, how precise and carefully worded is it? Where is it ambiguous, allowing for varied interpretations of the rules that might cause problems or, conversely, allowing for a proper and prudent flexibility? What we are looking for here is how a voice—all of the elements of diction, syntax, tone, and structure—conveys that sense that this is important, that these rules are to be obeyed, that there are precise instructions to be followed and consequences if they are broken.

Task 4.2

Read, slowly and carefully, the excerpt from the book of Deuteronomy (in the King James version) that follows. Pay attention to the style, the voice, and the interesting language in which the rules are structured. Look at macrostructure as well as microstructure.

Some background before you read:

These are, of course, the central rules for the Israelite community, which had recently escaped from slavery in Egypt and was now wandering across the desert in search of a new home, the "holy land" of Israel. According to the Bible, Moses went up on a mountain and brought them down on stone tablets. The Decalogue, or Ten Commandments, is only a small part of The Law, the Torah, the fundamental teaching of Judaism, which continues for some length after these fundamental statements. The selection, then, is from the book of Deuteronomy, chapter 5, verses 6–21.

⁶I am the Lord thy God, which brought thee out of the land of Egypt, from the house of bondage.

⁷Thou shalt have none other gods before me.

⁸Thou shalt not make thee any graven image, or any likeness of any thing that is in heaven above, or that is in the earth beneath, or that is in the waters beneath the earth:

⁹Thou shalt not bow down thyself unto them, nor serve them: for I the Lord thy God am a jealous God, visiting the iniquity of the fathers upon the children unto the third and fourth generation of them that hate me.

¹⁰And shewing mercy unto thousands of them that love me and keep my commandments.

¹¹Thou shalt not take the name of the Lord thy God in vain; for the Lord will not hold him guiltless that taketh his name in vain.

¹²Keep the Sabbath day to sanctify it, as the Lord thy God hath commanded thee.

¹³Six days thou shalt labour, and do all thy work:

¹⁴But the seventh day is the Sabbath of the Lord thy God: in it thou shalt not do any work, thou, nor thy son, nor thy daughter, nor thy manservant, nor thy maidservant, nor thine ox, nor thine ass, nor any of thy cattle, nor thy stranger that is within thy gates; that thy manservant and thy maidservant may rest as well as thou.

¹⁵And remember that thou wast a servant in the land of Egypt, and that the Lord thy God brought thee out thence through a mighty hand and by a stretched out arm: therefore the Lord thy God commanded thee to keep the Sabbath day.

¹⁶Honour thy father and thy mother, as the Lord God hath commanded thee; that thy days may be prolonged, and that it may go well with thee, in the land which the Lord thy God giveth thee.

¹⁷Thou shall not kill.

¹⁸Neither shalt thou commit adultery.

¹⁹Neither shalt thou steal.

²⁰Neither shalt thou bear false witness against thy neighbor.

²¹Neither shalt thou desire thy neighbor's wife, neither shalt thou covet thy neighbor's house, his field, or his manservant, or his maidservant, his ox, his ass, or any thing that is thy neighbour's.³

Task 4.3

Now, take your rules from Task 4.1 and rewrite them, imitating the style and structure of the King James Bible's Ten Commandments. Look at individual sentences and try to imitate their structure and vocabulary; further, try to capture the "rhythm" of the rules themselves—notice some are longer than others, and that there is an introduction to these rules. Consider point of view—who is saying this?

To complete this exercise, you will need to go back and re-read the biblical passage very carefully as you write. You should look at the large and small ways that this voice is created.

Look at the macrostructure *of Deuteronomic style; that is, notice the large blocks of structure that set up this voice. We've already hinted at one of them—the varying length and detail of each commandment. Look further: what happens first, second, and third in this passage? And as*

I hinted above, look at the speaker of this passage, or in other words the point of view in which this passage is written.

Look at the microstructure of the King James style. What little turns of phrase make this voice sound as it does? What sort of diction (that is, word choice or vocabulary) makes this sound so different? Are the sentences long and ornate, or are they short and concise? Are they full of similes and images and metaphors, or are they straightforward and flat? What other little things make up the sound of this voice? One thing you might notice here is the rhythm between positive and negative statements.

When you are done writing, bring your rules to class. Share them with two classmates. Read each other's imitations. Now, compare your rules to the original King James Version. What different features did your classmates notice and imitate in the original? How did changing the voice change the authority, the tone, and the clarity of the rules? Did putting the rules in this voice add clarity or create more ambiguity? What should be done about that? What else can you learn from their rules that you will want to include in your work? Make some notes for when you revise your rules.

Great Ideas: Torah, Law, Morality, and Culture

On what do we base our laws? What are laws for? These are significant questions that any society must answer. As in so many other things, the Western attitude to the law is a combination of the Judaic and the Greco-Roman notions.

The Jews were and are a people of the Law—the Torah. Their world is defined by the Law that Moses brought down from the mountain. After the choice of this people by God to be his chosen people, and the Exodus itself, the giving of the Law is one of the most significant events in Judaic history, and much of the rest of these first five books of the Bible is a listing and elaboration of these laws—laws for proper consumption of food, for how one is to treat another, for acting in the community. The people of God, then, are defined by the fact that their laws are not arbitrary—they come from God—and that *justice* is a crucial component of who they are, how they should act, and ultimately, how they relate to the divine and are saved as a people. In the New Testament, Jesus radically extends the law of Torah and claims to fulfill it. Law is relationship, but law is also a part of the natural order of things.

The Romans particularly saw themselves as a people of law, and the *Pax Romana* was seen as bringing order to the known world largely through bringing Roman law. Law here is opposed to lawlessness—that state where the strong have their own way simply because they can, where "might makes right," where bullies do as they like. Imagine a community in serious chaos, with no police force or government agency effectively present—for instance, after a serious natural disaster, a tsunami or hurricane—and you know the consequences of living without law: the physically strong, the armed, the violent, quickly attempt to impose their will upon others. (Given the experience of Roman occupation, and the excesses of Rome during the Imperial period, one could question whether Rome honored this idea of Roman law consistently, but that is a question for another time.) In the Roman conception, law exists precisely to bring order to this situation, to establish norms by which all must behave, and to punish those who would attempt to make might their right.

Interestingly, Roman law as organized late in the empire in the Code of Justinian is *positive* law; it defines the ideal situation in human behaviors and thus regulates failures to live up to these standards, which is why in this system, one is guilty until proven innocent. Many European countries still have Roman law as the basis of their system of justice. The system of law developed in the British Isles is quite different. Termed "Common Law," it appears only when some dispute comes to light; then one appeals to what has been done in the past about such a dispute—that is, the *precedents* of a given case—so that law builds up gradually over time, historically, keeping in memory the community's attitude towards these disputes. Law is not based in the abstract, as in Roman law, but in the lived legal memory of the community, and abstract principles are only arrived at after long community experience. In this system, then, unlike the Roman one, a person is innocent until proven guilty—you are free to do as you wish until it is shown you have violated the community's historical standards.

As an English colony, with an English legal system, the United States largely inherited the English Common Law system, but one could see the U.S. Constitution as being a kind of superstructure of Roman law at the fundamental level—a document which lays out the principles of how the society is set up, what freedoms are allowed, and how people will act. The tensions between these two form some of the most interesting tensions to study in the U.S. legal system.

Is law, however, merely a set of arbitrary conventions—a kind of unspoken agreement among members of a community to act in certain ways in order to make things work? Or is there such a thing as "natural law," real moral standards and strictures based on the makeup of the cosmos and on human nature, that everyone in all times and places can know, understand, and try to follow? Here we move into the relationship of law and morality. Most liberals argue that there is no such thing as natural law, that a good look around the varied cultures of the world would show that every culture has different standards of morality and legality. Conservatives on the whole argue for the existence of natural law, or one might say, *conscience*: that people all around the world can and do know what is right and wrong, that there is remarkable consistency among the laws and moralities of different cultures, legal systems, and religions, because human nature and the nature of the cosmos are consistently given. J. Budziszewski at the University of Texas is one who has argued forcefully for the concept of natural law, while many postmodern thinkers—not least among them Stanley Fish—have argued that law is simply a product of cultural discourse.

And it gets even more complicated than that, because *interpretation* is crucial to all of these traditions of law and even natural law. The Torah has never existed alone; it is, and always has been, the subject of the commentary of Torah scholars who debate and extend the basic precepts of the Torah. Roman law, especially as it comes through the Middle Ages, acquires many levels of "glossing"—again, interpretation and commentary—on the meaning and application of the law. English Common Law is almost by definition a continual commentary, interpretation, and reevaluation of the cases and principles that are precedents. And finally, at least since *Marbury vs. Madison*, the role of the higher courts in the United States has been to interpret the Constitution and the Bill of Rights, those surprisingly brief statements of general principles for the American Republic. Interpretation, commentary, glossing: these are not passive but active attempts to discover meaning, relevance, significance, principle.

These are not just abstract questions—they go to the heart of how one acts every day and the fundamental basis of one's culture. Many of the First Amendment questions of recent vintage debate how much the Founders thought the Constitution to be fundamentally Judeo-Christian in its outlook—how much, that is, our country is rooted in Judeo-Christian law, morality, values. And battles over nominations to the U.S. Supreme Court have become very bitter over the issue of the Constitution's "original meaning," and whether that meaning is knowable by us today, worth recovering at all, or applicable to modern life.

So we return to the Torah, which Moses presented not just as a nice set of standards for the Israelite community, but as *the* law, written on the hearts of those whom God has chosen. You might contemplate your own attitudes toward law as you work through this chapter.

ॐ

Now that you have attempted your own imitation, you might be interested in seeing a student's attempt at the same task. Here again is the work of Diana Fernandez, who has translated into Deuteronomic style the rules of a club you might know rather well. Now, attempting to imitate the Ten Commandments for any other group or setting is bound to call forth at least a bit of irony, humor, or parody, and Ms. Fernandez runs with that here. Notice how she uses the biblical style not just to capture the rules, but also to convey her own sly and humorous attitude towards this group.

I am the Leader and Creator of the Club, Mickey Mouse, who helped pioneer moving cartoon pictures by starring in *Steamboat Willie*.

Thou shalt always refer to the Leader and Creator as M-I-C-K-E-Y M-O-U-S-E Mickey Mouse whenever time allows it.

Thou shalt have none other cartoon icons before me.

And may all cartoon ducks, rabbits, dogs, farm animals, and underwater sea sponges be treated as cheap imitations.

Thou shalt become and give birth to media-addicted generations who shall buy my overpriced merchandise.

Thou shalt feel privileged to do so.

Thou shalt especially treat Donald Duck according to the third commandment.

Thou must not be jealous of Annette and her ethnic charm; all mouseketeers are created equal.

Thou shalt memorize the Mickey Mouse March.

Thou shalt come along and sing the song and join the jamboree.

Thou shalt smile.

Thou shalt laugh.

Thou shalt play.

Thou shalt embroider thy name on all articles of clothing.

Thou shalt not covet thy neighbor's ears.

Through the years we shalt all be friends, wherever we shalt be.

You might look at the ways Ms. Fernandez was successful as well as looking at the things she did not capture, ways in which you might be able to improve upon her performance. She is having fun here, working in the style and structure of the KJV but unable to take herself or her subject seriously. Nevertheless, in the fun she has learned a great deal about language, rhythm, and authority.

Task 4.4

Now revise your rules, trying to get them even closer to the King James model, trying to make your own voice sound more "biblical." You will probably have to read the text at least one more time as you write, poring over it carefully for features to imitate. Bring them to class to share with your classmates.

When you are done, again bring the revised rules to class. Work with fellow students, seeing what you changed, what you retained, and what you can still learn. Go back over the original model, studying which features you considered most important to the voice and which ones you decided to omit or vary. Were you able to convey your attitude toward these rules, as Diana Fernandez did? How did you establish the authority of your rules and of the rule-giver?

Interlude: you are an authority

Authority becomes important in many different kinds of writing—whether you are evaluating a new movie, proposing changes in an organization, or critiquing attitudes and actions. You will not be listened to as carefully in any of these situations unless you can show yourself as having some kind of authority to speak. How do you show your authority? Well, all other things being equal, you show it by demonstrating your knowledge of, and experience with, the subject. If you can describe how different camera angles affect a scene in a movie, or can distinguish a box-and-one basketball defense from a three-two, people will more likely listen to you on those subjects; if you have no idea what those mean, you are not as likely to be credible. (In the biblical passage above, Yahweh quickly establishes his authority by reminding the Israelites that he is, well, *God*, the creator of the universe, and that he rescued them from slavery in Egypt through a series of miracles.) Living in a college environment, surrounded by professors with advanced degrees, you may often find yourself feeling very unauthoritative, a novice at everything: history, literature, chemistry, sculpture, geology, agribusiness.

But that is simply not true; it is just that you are likely a novice at the particular academic subjects in which these professors have established their authority. Quick: list all of the hobbies, clubs, avocations, and organizations in which you have been involved for a number of years. You have probably just listed the areas in which, compared to the average American, you are at least something of an authority. If you have played clarinet, or soccer, or chess, or performed in *Antigone* or other plays, and done so seriously for a number of years, you have some degree of authority there; if you hunt every year, if you can tear apart a V-8 engine and put it back together, if you have danced a *pas de deux* in a production by a semiprofessional company, you can speak out of a deeper knowledge than most of us have on those subjects.

I know of a seventy-year-old woman, a stay-at-home mother all her life, who did not believe in her own expertise and authority. Let us set aside for a moment her authority on raising seven kids; therein she had enormous authoritative experience. But let us look at another of her realms of expertise. Because she had made quilts for decades, quilters from several counties came to consult with her about their own work. She was an enormously respected authority on the art of quilting and did not even realize it. I once had another student, a "nontraditional" twenty-nine year old who had washed out of college the first time and was quite unsure of himself, thinking he had little to say in this sometimes bewildering world of academia. Yet he was an avid hunter and knew more about his state's hunting regulations than anyone I had spoken to. He ended up writing an essay for my class proposing changes to hunting rules on local public lands, an essay whose specific proposals were later adopted by the city council.

Now, what good is your authority? Well, of course, when it comes to that memo, that proposal, that critique, you are at an advantage, for your argument will be more accepted because of your authority. But another advantage this gives you is in invention: you probably have many things to say about your favorite hobby, know the problems and controversies, and have opinions on what people should and should not do. You can probably generate literally dozens of topics to write about as you think about your favorite activities. Still, this knowledge is not enough unless you can convey your authority through your words, in language that confidently shows that you have knowledge and experience on which to base your claims.[4]

Task 4.5

Write in your journal about this experience. How did writing the rules in this King James voice make them different from rules as they exist in a "modern" voice? How did changing the voice and style change what you said and how you said it? What else did you learn from this exercise? Even if you never write in this voice again, what can you take away from what you did in these exercises?

Why We're Doing This

Language is often, though not always, about power—the power to make or persuade people to do what we want them to do, the power to set the boundaries for conduct, the power to set the penalties for violating the rules. We are talking, that is, about law. Law is about language, about words, and their power to denote, delimit, and define. Of course, law is not just about raw power; it is about justice and fairness. Societies live by the rule of law precisely because it (at least ideally) treats all equally. Communities without law are simply ruled by those with power and force; without laws, the biggest and the strongest simply do what they wish. Under the rule of law, however, even those who are weak have a chance at fair treatment. (Under the Soviet rule during the Cold War, the Eastern Bloc governments were enormously sensitive to creating the *appearance* of law, constantly trying to give a veneer of legality to their actions. A person arrested by the secret police was always arraigned "properly" before a tribunal and brought up on some sort of charges, no matter how false or absurd.) So it is important to consider how language gives us power and constrains power; it is important to think about how the *style* and *voice* of our language shape this power, and it is important to think about how we have to be precise and careful in our use of language, especially when we are creating the rules by which a community works. And it is important to begin practicing using such a voice, to begin gaining power with one's own words, and becoming more aware of how others' words gain power over us.

Extra Exercises for Those Want to Do More

Find and assemble still more sets of rules. Study them carefully. What makes them different? How do they approach the question of voice? Which are more effective, and why?

Consider a different kind of rules. These do not prescribe—that is, they do not tell us what to do and not to do; they merely describe, telling us what implicit "rules" people already follow. For instance, you might come upon someone who has written "the rules for modern American dating," telling how people behave. How are these descriptive rules different from the prescriptive rules? How does their language change based on this different purpose? And how can descriptive rules slowly become prescriptive? Imitate one of these sets, writing your own set of descriptive rules.

Reflection

How You Can Build Beginnings Out of Nothing

N othing can come from nothing," King Lear says to his daughter Cordelia, and except for God, he's theologically correct: only Yahweh creates *ex nihilo*. And this is what terrifies so many writers, sending even some of the greats to the bottle or drugs: the fear of that blank page, the worry that one must write *something*, today, or by Thursday, or for next week, and nothing is forthcoming from the cracked pate. We've all been there, stricken for a time with Writer's Block, dread curse.

But now that you have worked through part 1 of this book, you not only have some of the best ways to describe and define; you also have some of the fundamental methods of what the classical rhetoricians called *inventio*, invention, or to use contemporary language, "finding a topic." You don't create from nothing, but you now do have tools to help you get a start on what you have to write. You didn't notice? Well, let's take a look at the invention techniques you now have at your disposal:

1. Description: one of the best ways to get topics for anything—an essay, an article, a talk to give to a group—is simply to begin by describing, accurately rendering the reality you see before you. That is, you can:

Describe a person, or a fictional character, or an important historical figure. By doing this, starting by accurately describing Odysseus or President Reagan or Isaac Newton or Brunelleschi or your classmate during the recent debate on Platonic Forms, you simply begin finding your subject matter. In a literary paper, if you carefully, accurately describe a character, you begin to enter into the questions, problems, thematic resonances, and troubles this character comes to represent. The same goes for contemporary or historical figures.

Describe an action or a narrative, which is a set of actions occurring over time. Again, whether you are describing a chemical process or an environmental catastrophe, Book Twenty-Two of the Iliad *or a slave's battle for freedom, the ability to describe actions can open up for you the questions you might explore later, either in this narrative form or in an explanatory or argumentative piece.*

But you can do more, if you expand just a bit. You can use these techniques to describe a problem or question and how you came to grapple with it, thus expanding from concrete tactile description into describing ideas, consequences, problems, controversies.

At any rate, accurate description—of a problem, a person, or an action—is often the first doorway into thinking about it fruitfully. For if you do not really know and see the subject before you, how can you accurately engage with it?

2. Definition: The classical rhetoricians prized this as one of the fundamental techniques of invention. For by defining something—honor, the tax code, supply as opposed to demand, tragedy—you engage, as we saw, in both the general and the specific, and often come to see the questions and problems that emerge once you have a clear idea of the terms involved.

&

Now, will this description make it into the final essay you write for your history or literature or physics class? Does the defined term, or the effort at definition, need to be the focus of your paper? Not necessarily, but it might indeed. What is important at this stage is that you have these techniques at your disposal for getting started, for making beginnings, for getting words, people, actions, terms, down on the page that you can then push around, organize, and eventually relate to others.

Part Two: Precision Tools and Finer Crafts

Chapter Five

Voices of Logic: Making Sense

*I*n the first section of this book, I wanted you to learn how to render, in words, the world around you, as well as the world inside you. You learned how to describe external reality and how to relate the internal reality of your thoughts in words by describing, defining, inquiring. Then we began working on using words in ways to discover the truth of things by defining concepts clearly, seeing things as they are, and using that clear sense to convey to others the truths we know or have found. So as the first section of the book has proceeded, we have begun directing our attention out to others, learning how to influence others, how to develop our authority in words, and how to set clear distinctions.

In this section we will begin refining those skills with particular respect to persuading others. One of the chief tools in communicating with others is logic. Logic could be defined in two ways: as "the rules for discovering the truth" and as "the rules for making sense to others." When we write to ourselves, we can make intuitive or associative leaps in our thought, because we ourselves understand where we are going and what we are thinking. Yet often it is important to be logical even to ourselves, so we can clearly arrive at the truth. And when we write to others, they *must* be able to follow our thoughts, and often they need to understand how we arrived at our terminating points and judgments. Logic, that is, enables us both to discover what is correct and to say things so that others can make sense of them and follow us to the truth. When we use logic, we set up our statements so that preliminary statements lead to the conclusions. When someone says to you that what you argue "doesn't make sense," he is accusing you of being *illogical*, of not following the procedures by which we show that our conclusions come from our previous statements.

And logic—just so you see where I am headed in these next few chapters—is one of the crucial tools of persuasion, of the ability to get others to agree with your views, to come over to your side. (It is not the *only* tool, as we will see later, but one of the crucial ones.) So a good persuasive writer must know something of how to make a logical argument.

Aristotle was one of the first who laid out the rules by which we can "make sense," or be logical, some 2,500 years ago. But again, rather than first teaching you in an abstract way Aristotle's rules of logic—the different forms of syllogism, the square of opposition, the kinds of logical fallacies, and so forth—I am interested at this point that you learn by doing: developing a logical argument, seeing how a logical argument might be structured.

To do that, we are going to take you this time to one of the great ages of logic in the Western tradition—indeed, in all of world culture: the High Middle Ages, the time of Scholasticism. You may think of, and have been taught, that the Middle Ages were an age of faith, but they were equally an age with a deep belief in the tools of logic and logical argumentation. This is called the age of the Scholastics because this practice was rooted in the advanced schools—the universities, a new form of school that developed in Europe at the end of the twelfth and beginning of the thirteenth centuries.

Class in a medieval university was often conducted by the method of the "Disputed Question." The Master (that is, someone with a master's degree) or Doctor (which just means "teacher"—the term comes from *docere*, "to lead out" of ignorance) would set before the class some question, such as, "Has the universe always existed or can we conclude from logic that it must have been created?" or "What is the proper relation of philosophy to theology?" or "Is drunkenness a sin?" (yes, this was apparently debated, and might be worth considering . . .). The

Master would arbitrarily divide the class in two, assigning sides in the debate to each group, and the two sides would debate the question, each taking a side, offering arguments and authorities for its side. A student may have to argue for or against a proposition, no matter his personal beliefs. At the end of class, the Master would make his *determinatio*, his summing up of the debate and his conclusions about the true answer to the question. Then, after telling the class the question for next time, he would dismiss them to prepare for the next class's disputed question.

As you can see, it was a form of education that prized and deeply trained the students in logical argumentation and debate. We will borrow from that technique and have you participate in a Disputed Question of your own making.

Task 5.1

Use your invention techniques to come up with a Disputed Question that you would like to consider for this assignment. It can be a deeply philosophical question ("Was the universe created?") or a political question ("Should the United States keep troops in the Middle East?" or "Should the government sanction same-sex unions?") or a question of ethics and morals ("Is abortion wrong in all cases?"). You might want to brainstorm ten questions and pick one, or free-write about issues you believe to be important.[1]

Next, sketch out in your own, free-writing voice, your answer to your question. What reasons do you have for your answer? What opposing arguments in the debate might you have to refute?

As always, bring the completed work to class and share it with two classmates. This time, ask them to be antagonists against your side of the argument, whether they actually agree or disagree with what you are saying. Where do they find your reasons insufficient? What opposing views did you forget to include? Make notes of these so you can use them to improve your arguments.

Task 5.2

Read, slowly and carefully, the selection below from the *Summa Theologica* of Thomas Aquinas. It will help to read it out loud, and I recommend this strongly. If there are words you have not encountered, look up their meanings. Take notes on the reading.

First, put into your own words what Aquinas is saying;

Second, note the interesting ways he goes about saying these things. What structures does he employ? That is, in what order does he put the different parts of his argument? What does he do with sentence structure, with his diction? How does he incorporate others' views? What does he leave out?

Some background before you read:

Thomas Aquinas (Tomaso d'Aquino—he was born in a castle south of Rome near the town of Aquino) was one of the most important philosophers in world history. A theologian whose thought forms the backbone of a great deal of Roman Catholic theology, he is a significant figure in any history of world thought. Living in the thirteenth century, he saw as his grand project reconciling the truths of the great classical (and thus non-Christian) philosophers with the truths of Christian revelation. His works cover vast ground, touching on and examining in detail virtually every fundamental question of ancient philosophy and fundamental questions in Christian theology. Though many of his ideas were quite controversial in his own lifetime, he was canonized in 1323—less than fifty years after his death—and named "The Angelic Doctor" by Pope Pius V in 1567. He was at core a teacher: he learned from his master, Albert the Great, at the University of Cologne, and then he himself went on to teach at the University of Paris and other schools. He therefore was one who participated on a day-to-day basis in the scholastic teaching method I outlined above. As you read the selection below, notice how his presentation borrows from, or even embodies, that form of teaching by debate.

The question asked here entails what has come to be known as Just War Theory. Given the New Testament's message of humility, forgiveness, and peacefulness (as in "turning the other cheek"), is it ever allowable for a Christian, or a Christian nation, to engage in war? And if so, under what conditions? This of course is no abstract, academic question, and has come to the fore once again because of the events of September 11, 2001, the Iraq War, and the responses, both rhetorical and military, that have followed. Aquinas takes up this question and considers it carefully in the following passage.[2]

Read slowly and carefully; Aquinas is expecting you to consider the logic of his arguments with great care.

Question 40. Whether it is always sinful to wage war?

Objection 1: It would seem that it is always sinful to wage war. Because punishment is not inflicted except for sin. Now those who wage war are threatened by Our Lord with punishment, according to Mt. 26:52: "All that take the sword shall perish with the sword." Therefore all wars are unlawful.

Objection 2: Further, whatever is contrary to a Divine precept is a sin. But war is contrary to a Divine precept, for it is written (Mt. 5:39): "But I say to you not to resist evil"; and (Rm. 12:19): "Not revenging yourselves, my dearly beloved, but give place unto wrath." Therefore war is always sinful.

Objection 3: Further, nothing, except sin, is contrary to an act of virtue. But war is contrary to peace. Therefore war is always a sin.

Objection 4: Further, the exercise of a lawful thing is itself lawful, as is evident in scientific exercises. But warlike exercises which take place in tournaments are forbidden by the Church, since those who are slain in these trials are deprived of ecclesiastical burial. Therefore it seems that war is a sin in itself.

On the contrary, Augustine says in a sermon on the son of the centurion: "If the Christian Religion forbade war altogether, those who sought salutary advice in the Gospel would rather have been counseled to cast aside their arms, and to give up soldiering altogether. On the contrary, they were told: 'Do violence to no man . . . and be content with your pay.' If he commanded them to be content with their pay, he did not forbid soldiering."

I answer that, in order for a war to be just, three things are necessary. First, the authority of the sovereign by whose command the war is to be waged. For it is not the business of a private individual to declare war, because he can seek for redress of his rights from the tribunal of his superior. Moreover it is not the business of a private individual to summon together the people, which has to be done in wartime. And as the care of the common weal is committed to those who are in authority, it is their business to watch over the common weal of the city, kingdom or province subject to them. And just as it is lawful for them to have recourse to the sword in defending that common weal against internal disturbances, when they punish evil-doers, according to the words of the Apostle (Rm. 13:4): "He beareth not the sword in vain: for he is God's minister, an avenger to execute wrath upon him that doth evil"; so too, it is their business to have recourse to the sword of war in defending the common weal against external enemies. Hence it is said to those who are in authority (Ps. 81:4): "Rescue the poor: and deliver the needy out of the hand of the sinner"; and for this reason Augustine says (*Contra Faust.* xxii, 75): "The natural order conducive to peace among mortals demands that the power to declare and counsel war should be in the hands of those who hold the supreme authority."

Secondly, a just cause is required, namely that those who are attacked, should be attacked because they deserve it on account of some fault. Wherefore Augustine says (QQ. in Hept., qu. x, super Jos.): "A just war is wont to be described as one that avenges wrongs, when a nation or state has to be punished, for refusing to make amends for the wrongs inflicted by its subjects, or to restore what it has seized unjustly."

Thirdly, it is necessary that the belligerents should have a rightful intention, so that they intend the advancement of good, or the avoidance of evil. Hence Augustine says (*De Verb. Dom.*): "True religion looks upon as peaceful those wars that are waged not for motives of aggrandizement, or cruelty, but with the object of securing peace, of punishing evil-doers, and of uplifting the good." For it may happen that the war is declared by the legitimate authority, and for a just cause, and yet be rendered unlawful through a wicked intention. Hence Augustine says (*Contra Faust.* xxii, 74): "The passion for inflicting harm, the cruel thirst for vengeance, an unpacific and relentless spirit, the fever of revolt, the lust of power, and such like things, all these are rightly condemned in war."

Reply to Objection 1: As Augustine says (*Contra Faust.* xxii, 70): "To take the sword is to arm oneself in order to take the life of anyone, without the command or permission of superior or lawful authority." On the other hand, to have recourse to the sword (as a private person) by the authority of the sovereign or judge, or (as a public person) through zeal for justice, and by the authority, so to speak, of God, is not to "take the sword," but to use it as commissioned by another, wherefore it does not deserve punishment. And yet even those who make sinful use of the sword are not always slain with the sword, yet they always perish with their own sword, because, unless they repent, they are punished eternally for their sinful use of the sword.

Reply to Objection 2: Such like precepts, as Augustine observes (*De Serm. Dom. in Monte* i, 19), should always be borne in readiness of mind, so that we be ready to obey them, and, if necessary, to refrain from resistance or self-defense. Nevertheless it is necessary sometimes for a man to act otherwise for the common good, or for the good of those with whom he is fighting. Hence Augustine says (*Ep. ad Marcellin.* cxxxviii): "Those whom we have to punish with a kindly severity, it is necessary to handle in many ways against their will. For when we are stripping a man of the lawlessness of sin, it is good for him to be vanquished, since nothing is more hopeless than the happiness of sinners, whence arises a guilty impunity, and an evil will, like an internal enemy."

Reply to Objection 3: Those who wage war justly aim at peace, and so they are not opposed to peace, except to the evil peace, which Our Lord "came not to send upon earth" (Mt. 10:34). Hence Augustine says (*Ep. ad Bonif.* clxxxix): "We do not seek peace in order to be at war, but we go to war that we may have peace. Be peaceful, therefore, in warring, so that you may vanquish those whom you war against, and bring them to the prosperity of peace."

Reply to Objection 4: Manly exercises in warlike feats of arms are not all forbidden, but those which are inordinate and perilous, and end in slaying or plundering. In olden times warlike exercises presented no such danger, and hence they were called "exercises of arms" or "bloodless wars," as Jerome states in an epistle.[3]

Task 5.3

Now, take your argument from Task 5.1 and rewrite it, arguing your case in the voice and structure of Aquinas's scholastic argumentation. Try to imitate his diction, syntax, and macrostructure. See if you can present it like a question, deal with objections, and provide an answer. Try not merely to echo the style of this argument, but to make a clear and truthful argument yourself.

To complete this assignment, you will need to go back and re-read the selection very carefully as you write. You will need to look at the large and small ways that Aquinas creates this "voice."

> Look at the macrostructure *of Aquinas's style; that is, notice the large blocks of structure that set up this voice. What happens first, second, and third? Does he take up his own views first? Where does he include the views of*

those who disagree with him? How and where does he answer their views?

Look at the microstructure of Aquinas's scholastic voice. What little turns of phrase make this voice sound as it does? What sort of diction (that is, word choice or vocabulary) makes this sound so different? Are the sentences long and ornate, or are they short and concise? Are they full of similes and images and metaphors, or are they straightforward and flat? Does the writing refer to or allude to other writings? What other details make up the sound of this voice? Try to do what those things do.

You will need to think very carefully about your own position and the opposing position in your argument. What are the fundamental principles on which you base your argument? What are the logical steps by which you arrive at your conclusions? If it helps, return briefly to chapter 3 to ensure that you define carefully any terms you use.

Bring the logical arguments back to class. Read them aloud to classmates. Which features did you capture that your partners did not? Are there some things your partners noticed and were able to capture that you were not able to capture? Do your partners find your arguments logical? Did you represent the opposing side's position accurately? Did you answer the objections well?

Did you find this type of writing more challenging than other assignments in this book? Why? Many people find that this assignment challenges them in two ways: finding careful reasons for their point of view, and imagining the other side's objections to their point of view. Both, as you see, require your *imagination*, not just your logical facility. Your logical facility must discipline your thinking, making good definitions and distinctions between terms, leading carefully from one thought to the next.

Take a look at how one student imitated the Aquinas proof in a literature class I was teaching. We had been reading the *Odyssey*, that tale of Odysseus's travels and attempts to get home to his faithful wife, Penelope, after the Trojan War. As he travels, the poem constantly compares his future homecoming (the Greek word for homecoming is *nostos*; the plural is *nostoi*) to that of Agamemnon, the leader of the Greeks, who was murdered by his wife Klytaimnestra (and in some versions, her lover, Aigisthos) upon *his* return home. Clearly Klytaimnestra, the treacherous wife, serves as a foil for Penelope, the faithful wife. But Peter Bauman asks if Klytaimnestra or Helen of Troy, the cause of the Trojan War (she left her husband Menelaos to be with Paris, the Trojan), is the real foil for Penelope. Watch how he imitates the Thomistic proof in order to make his point about this great epic.

Question LXXI
On the Major Women in the *Iliad* and the *Odyssey*
(In One Article)
We must next consider the major women in The *Iliad* and The *Odyssey*, under which head there is one point of inquiry: (I) Whether Helen or Klytaimnestra serves as a foil for Penelope?
First Article
Whether Helen serves as a foil for Penelope?
We proceed thus to the First Article:—
Objection 1. It would seem that she is not because Klytaimnestra would serve as a better foil for Penelope. For Klytaimnestra betrays her husband, Agamemnon, at the end of his long nostos, contrasting Penelope's faithfulness to Odysseus. Therefore Klytaimnestra serves as a foil for Penelope.
Obj. 2. Further, Helen does not serve as a good foil for Penelope because she never willingly betrays Menelaos. But she merely acts under the gods' influence, while Klytaimnestra acted within her own power. Mortals are always more responsible for their actions when there are no outside forces influencing them. Penelope, too, does not act under the influence of the gods. Therefore, Klytaimnestra serves as a better foil for Penelope than Helen does.

On the contrary, Helen serves as the more perfect foil for Penelope in *The Iliad* and *The Odyssey*.

I answer that, Helen, as opposed to Klytaimnestra, is the better foil for Penelope in three ways, their opposite qualities, the two different webs that they weave, and their opposite journeys. Firstly, because it is through Helen's "terrible wildness" and forgetfulness that she is "stirred to do the shameful thing [that] she / [does]" (*Odyssey* XXIII, 222–24). But this is contrasted to the wisdom and prudence of Penelope, who first tests Odysseus when he reveals himself to her, so as not to be mistaken or fooled by the gods or man alike. For instance, so wise is Penelope and so prudent, that even though she can "look him straight in the face" and see that he appears to be Odysseus, she still does not trust her senses. On the contrary, she tests him, believing that "if he is truly Odysseus, / and he has come home, then [they] will find other ways, and better, / to recognize each other" (*Odyssey* XXIII, 197–99). "For always the spirit deep in [her] very heart was fearful / that some one of mortal men would come [her] way and deceive [her] / with words" (*Odyssey* XXIII, 215–17). On the contrary, Helen displays her forgetfulness in Book IV of *The Odyssey*, when she gives Telemachus "a medicine / of heartsease, free of gall, to make one forget all sorrows" (*Odyssey* IV, 220–21). For Homer is attempting to show that Helen has a propensity for forgetting things. For Homer contrasts this, later in Book IV, with Penelope's repetition of the phrase: "first I lost a husband with the heart of a lion / and who among the Danaans surpassed in all virtues, / and great, whose fame goes wide," a phrase which Homer uses to show that Odysseus, even after twenty long years, is always on Penelope's mind. Hence, Homer shows that Penelope possesses the opposite qualities of Helen.

Secondly, the webs that Helen and Penelope weave in the *Iliad* and the *Odyssey* shed light on their relationship. For in Book III of *The Iliad* Helen weaves "a red folding robe, working into it the numerous struggles / of Trojans, breakers of the horses, and bronze-armoured Achaians, / struggles that they endured for her sake" (*Iliad* III, 126–28). Helen is thus glorifying the war that she caused through her recklessness and wildness by creating a constant reminder of it for everybody to see. On the contrary, Penelope's robe, "a shroud for hero Laertes, for when the destructive / doom of death which lays men low shall take him" (*Odyssey* II, 99–100) is simply "another stratagem of her heart's devising" (II, 93). Hence, while Penelope uses her web to trick the suitors, "since she is so dowered with the wisdom bestowed by Athene" (*Odyssey* II, 116), Helen's web serves to amplify her own foolishness and recklessness. Since wisdom is the opposite of recklessness, Helen is a foil for Penelope.

Thirdly, Helen's literal journey from Greece to Troy is the inverse of Penelope's figurative journey, in which she accompanies Odysseus from Troy to Greece. For Penelope's journey becomes evident in the epic simile in Book XXIII of the *Odyssey*, stating:

> As when land appears welcome to men who are swimming,
> After Poseidon has smashed their strong-built ship on the open
> Water, pounding it with the weight of wind and the heavy
> Seas, and only a few escape the gray water landward
> By swimming, with a thick surf of salt coated upon them,
> And gladly they set foot on the shore, escaping the evil;
> So welcome was her husband to her as she looked upon him,
> And she could not let him go from the embrace of her white arms (233–40)

Hence, Homer compares in the simile the literal journey of Odysseus with the figurative journey of Penelope, a journey marked by her faithfulness, prudence, and wisdom along the way in waiting for Odysseus to return and handling the suitors. On the contrary, Helen's journey, brought about by her faithlessness, wildness, and recklessness is literally the opposite of the journey that both Penelope and

Odysseus make together. Therefore, the opposite natures of these journeys serve to show the opposite characters of Penelope and Helen, making each a foil for the other.

Reply Obj 1. While at first glance or without proper inspection Klytaimnestra might appear to be the better foil for Penelope, however, the two poems do not justify this with evidence or support. The contrasting evidence between Helen and Penelope is clear. Hence Helen is a better foil for Penelope than Klytaimnestra.

Reply Obj 2. Precisely the fact that the gods trick and fool Helen and not Penelope serves to display the recklessness and foolishness of Helen. If she were more wise, witty, or prudent, then she would never have allowed the gods to trick her. Hence the Greeks and Trojans fight an entire war because of recklessness and foolishness, further showing Homer's disdain for these two qualities. On the contrary, Klytaimnestra uses trickery against her husband, similar to what Penelope does, but to a much lesser degree, obviously. Hence Penelope and Klytaimnestra do not possess as many opposing qualities as a transitory reading of the poem might presume. For Helen and Penelope do possess many opposing qualities. Therefore Helen is the better foil for Penelope.

Task 5.4

Now revise your scholastic argument based on your discussions with your fellow students. Try to be even more precise in the terms you use; try to be more logical, and include more of the features of Aquinas's voice.

I find it both interesting and important that this form states the opposing views—the "Objections"—first. This structure foregrounds the fact that the question is *disputed*, and it forces the one arguing to deal with his opponents in a sympathetic way first. Like walking a mile in someone else's moccasins, the scholastic method pushes one towards considering that, if we wish to be successful in an argument, we must deal with those who disagree with us.

Great Ideas: Aquinas and Einstein, Occam and Heisenberg, Faith and Logic

The medieval love of logic was not grounded in sentimentality; it was grounded in faith, and this faith in the applicability and usefulness of logic as a tool for discovering truth has had far-reaching consequences for Western and indeed world culture.

How can logic be grounded in faith? Well, consider the following series of statements:

୬ *God is infinitely rational; He is Reason itself.*

୬ *Therefore, when He created the cosmos (the universe), He acted rationally.*

୬ *Therefore, the cosmos He created is rational, logical; it is not a haphazard or irrational place.*

୬ *As a result, humans can use their reason to explore the universe, understand it, and thereby understand something about the Creator who created it.*

Interesting, no? Once one posits God as infinitely rational, the conclusions come logically: our reason is a tool to discover the fundamentally logical workings of the world around us. That is, we can investigate the world rationally, using the tools of logic to see how things add up, how they make sense—why planets move the way they do in the sky, how DNA works, or how the particles in different kinds of atoms behave (and how many there are), for instance.

Medieval thinkers thereby often described the cosmos as a text, a book that could be "read" by those who learned to study it carefully. Alan of Lille, a philosopher and teacher at the school at Chartres Cathedral in the twelfth century, put it this way:

Omnis mundi creatura
Quasi liber et pictura
Nobis est in speculum

(All the things of the world appear to us as in a mirror, like a book or a picture.)

That is, things—trees, rocks, a river, the flight of a sparrow, the stars in the sky—are like pictures or books, and if you can train yourself by the tools of logical investigation to study them carefully, you can learn to "read" this book of nature and understand its meaning. This is why Thomas Aquinas is so careful, and so thorough, in his philosophic investigations: he is "reading the book of nature" carefully so as to learn something of the ultimate. As a model, a master, for careful, logical thinking, one could do worse than apprentice oneself to Thomas Aquinas.

This faith both in God's rational universe and the power of reason to discover the underlying truths of the cosmos undergirds modern science. That may seem ironic, but it is better to say it is a paradox: faith leads to science in Western culture. For if we think about it for a moment, "science" doesn't work unless the universe makes sense. We cannot test with experiments, or repeat results, and we definitely cannot draw out "theories" and "laws" about the behavior of stars, atoms, forces, or a monkey's genes, unless we presume first that the universe *makes sense*, is logical and rational at its deepest core. Unless a biologist believes that, at base, genes will obey logical laws about how atoms and molecules interact, he is chasing ephemera and wasting his time. So in many ways, it is the science departments of modern universities—often more than the literature, history, or art departments—which have retained the fundamental faith of medieval culture.

Many histories of science overlook the Middle Ages or give it scant attention, because *experimental* science itself is not really born until the intellectual movement historians for a while have called the Renaissance, in the age which now we term the Early Modern period. But the philosophical—or theological, if you will—roots of science are born in the High Middle Ages, in this faith in God as rational. And so one of the greatest innovations of Western culture—and the one that arguably has had the most immediate impact on humans' lives all over the globe—has its roots in this scholastic moment.

Over the last century, physicists who study matter at its most fundamental level—the protons, neutrons, electrons, and then even smaller quarks and leptons—have come to challenge the medieval view that the universe is rational. One of the great debates of twentieth-century science was begun by Werner Heisenberg, famous for his "uncertainty principle," and Albert Einstein, author of the theory of relativity. You might be surprised to know that the theory of relativity does not say that everything is relative, but quite the opposite: it explains what is absolutely true in all frames of reference. Einstein said famously, "God does not throw dice," defending the medieval idea that the universe is rational because made by a rational God. To this Heisenberg responded: "Is it our place to prescribe to God how he is to make his universe?" In saying this, Heisenberg was echoing, by the way, the late-medieval philosopher William of Occam, whose theory of nominalism was a crucial step towards experimental science. Occam believed that to say "God is reason, and therefore he was constrained to create rationally when he made the universe," is to put limits on an all-powerful God, who could have chosen to make any kind of universe He pleased—a rational one or an irrational one. And Stephen Barr, writing in 2007 in *First Things*, if I understand him correctly, says that Einstein tried to preserve a "deterministic" Newtonian universe of material causes, whereas quantum mechanics opens up a more complex universe of human freedom and interpenetration of mind and matter. The questions, that is, of faith and reason, the structure of the cosmos and God's action, are hardly insignificant old "angels-on-a-pin"-type problems.

Task 5.7

Write a few paragraphs reflecting on what you've learned in these exercises. How has this assignment made you more aware of the methods we use to debate? How has it improved your ability to make careful distinctions and argue logically?

Why We're Doing This

As I said above, the ancient Greeks saw logic as a tool—a tool for discovering truth. You can learn to use this tool, too, if you practice with it by imitating logical arguments. By forcing yourself to put your thoughts in this seemingly mechanical, syllogistic, and scholastic structure, you can develop a sense of logical structure in your writing. You are not likely ever to write again in this very specialized structure; a business memo argues its points in different kinds of paragraphs. But practice with scholastic argumentation can spill over into other forms of writing, encouraging you to make more careful distinctions and argue more logically, as well as deal with others' objections to your arguments. And again, by asking you to write in this *very* different form, I am hoping to stretch your writing muscles in new and fascinating directions.

If you do wish to learn more about the rules of formal logic, there are many textbooks you can consult; check your library. Or see a philosophy or mathematics professor; perhaps you can take a class in logic.

Extra Exercises for Those Who Want to Do More

Take a typical column from the editorial page of your daily newspaper. These pieces try to argue a point. Recast it in the form of a scholastic Disputed Question. Does the writing deal with a clear, and clearly worded, question? Does the piece argue its points clearly? Does it handle objections to its position? Does it argue its own points logically?

Try to arrange a Disputed Question debate in one of your classes, based on the methods outlined in this chapter. Or arrange for one in public over some important issue in your campus community.

Chapter Six

Voices of Argument:
Persuading Others[1]

*I*n the last chapter, you practiced proving, logically, a point you had to make. The medieval Scholastics would have said this use of logic was the best method for discovering truth. However, you could think of it in another way: as a way to persuade others of what you have found to be the truth. (The difference here is between the skills of dialectic, or logic, and rhetoric.) So you could say that in the previous chapter we studied one way of assembling an argument—the extremely structured, careful, logical argumentation style of the medieval schoolmen. If you learned that well, you saw how attempting to convince someone of a point can be a very detailed, careful matter indeed. You probably are not going to write, or talk, like that very often in your life, with that sort of logical precision. But one of the things we constantly do with words is attempt to persuade someone to agree with us. Yes, we do it all the time: we try to persuade the university to build more parking lots; we try to persuade others that an album we like by our favorite pop group is really quite an artistic achievement; we attempt to persuade the city council to change the zoning laws; we try to persuade our professors that we really deserved a better grade. In this chapter, I am actually going to take you further back in time from the Middle Ages to the time of ancient Rome, when one of the greatest persuaders of all time worked in the courts and in the Senate of Rome.

His name was Marcus Tullius Cicero, and he was one of the outstanding public figures of his day—a literate lawyer, a philosophical writer and commentator on the public scene, an outspoken senator who believed in the republican system of ancient Rome and who fought tyranny wherever he saw it, and a lover of the arts and literature. Because most of his career focused on persuading people through words—especially speeches—he stands in the Western tradition as one of the great rhetoricians of all time. He not only created great persuasive arguments that people still read, admire, and study; he wrote guides to rhetoric and gave the basic form to the persuasive argument (and, not incidentally, the academic essay) that writers still use today.[2]

A word or two about the terms *rhetoric* and *rhetorician.* Most of the time we encounter the word *rhetoric* in a negative context today; it tends to have the adjective "empty" before it and apply to politicians' ways of saying words that mean nothing. People on the campaign trail, and journalists on talk shows, are always talking about "the empty rhetoric" of this or that politician. But this is a debased form of a word with a rich positive tradition in Western thought. Rhetoric is a Greek term that, simply put, means the art of persuasion—the art, or technique, of using your words to convince others to agree with your views. Its early history has a high point around 300 B.C. with Aristotle, who wrote one of the first guides to the principles of this art, but studies of this art actually began more than one hundred years before that, when the Sophists, a group of teachers in Athens, taught young men the techniques of speaking and persuasion (and became the objects of Socrates' and Plato's scorn). Rhetoric has been one of the "seven liberal arts" for more than two millennia—one of the crucial things to study in order to become educated. The very fact that most colleges have a mandatory requirement in something like "composition" is a survival of this long-running part of the curriculum, and the person who runs such a program today usually has a Ph.D. in something like "rhetoric and composition."

A word or two about *arguing* and *argumentation.* Many people have a negative connotation of these words as well. Arguing, to many, means people shouting, getting heated—the kind of thing teenagers do with their parents, spouses do before a divorce, or two lovers do when the relationship is on the skids. But when we use these terms in the context of rhetoric, we simply mean by "arguing" the idea of "putting together your thoughts in a way that will be persuasive," and "an argument" is what results when you do this. When we try to persuade someone, we do not try to *make* the person agree by overpowering them; we try to *persuade* them that the reasonable thing to do is to agree. As a student of mine said once after writing a paper: "I wanted my audience to read my paper and *want* to change their minds . . . not because I beat them into it, but because I've presented the evidence so that they realize they *should* agree with me." If you think of argument this way, you probably can see why a parent shouting at a teenager is not usually a very effective rhetorical strategy for persuading her not to date that guy with the multiple piercings and the naked-women tattoos.

Also, a few words about *opinions* and arguing. In the United States recently, we have developed a kind of mantra: "Everyone is entitled to his or her own opinion." And that is true; it is one of the fundamental principles of a democratic system of government. However, this does not necessarily mean that everyone's opinion is correct, or equally worthwhile. I may have the opinion that it is a dry, sunny day; if it is raining outside, I suppose I am still entitled to that opinion, *but that opinion is wrong.* (Of course, it's really not a statement of opinion anyway, but these days we seem to confuse statements of fact with "having one's own opinion.") Or again: we probably all know people, unfortunately, who hold racist or stereotypical opinions such as "Asians are bad drivers" or "Norwegians are all dim-witted." In our democracy, people are entitled by the First Amendment to express those opinions. But of course such totalizing opinions are *wrong.* How do we know they are wrong? Because we can prove them wrong by citing evidence—copious evidence!—to the contrary. You see, we seem to have developed an idea in America that we should all just let each other keep our own opinions—because no one can tell you your opinions are wrong. But of course we *can*, in many, if not most, cases.

Furthermore, we have developed an idea that it is the *nice* thing to do to be tolerant, to let people have their own opinions, and that it is mean and unkind to try to change people's opinions. But think about that for a minute. If you have a friend who is an alcoholic, and he has the opinion that it is okay to drink three cases of beer each day, which is the nice, kind thing to do—let him continue in this self-destructive error, or try to change his opinion? Surely a true friend would try to *persuade* him he is wrong, that he needs to get help. Or what if a friend told you she planned to commit suicide? Or that she was having unprotected sex with multiple partners? Should you let her continue in these actions because *hey, it's her opinion* that this is a good thing? Surely not. And the same goes for a university, a community, or our nation: if we feel the country is going down a wrong path, is it not our *duty* to discuss, to argue, to try to persuade others to do things differently? A democracy only works if we all believe that we can and should try to talk together, argue with one another amicably, about what should be done, and come to some agreements about what should be done. So, please, no more of this "it is just his opinion" nonsense. Instead, when someone states an opinion, ask him or her, "Why do you think that?" or "Do you have any evidence that your view is correct?"—and expect people to do the same to you. As the great twentieth-century rhetorical thinker Richard Weaver noted, ideas have consequences, which is why we should be so careful about them. And as my colleague Scott Crider has written in his book *The Office of Assertion*, rhetoric is the art of soul-leading, of taking someone to a richer, more truthful place than he heretofore has been.

Back to Cicero and ancient Rome. To understand why rhetoric was so important at that time, you have to understand something about the law courts in the ancient world. When there was a dispute—whether it was a criminal or a civil case—there were at first no professional lawyers, no "evidence." All that happened was that you stood up and told your side of the story, and then your opponent stood up and told his side of the story. The judge or jury would listen to both, decide who was in the right, and render a judgment. (Think of the TV show *The People's*

Court and you will get a rough picture of how cases were handled.) Now, in this type of legal system, you can surely see how the ability to be persuasive—to speak coherently, logically, convincingly—was a crucial skill to have. And pretty soon, people who could not speak very well started hiring lawyers—stand-in speakers—to speak for them. This was Cicero's profession; as a great and persuasive speaker, one who knew the principles of how to persuade and could apply them in practice, he was soon in high demand as a lawyer to speak on behalf of others.

And a great deal of the way we talk about rhetoric today still comes from this art's background in the law courts. We try to "win" an argument; we try to "defeat" our opponents. We try to "make a case" or "prove our case" for why smoking should be banned in public places, or marijuana should or should not be legalized. We have to deal not only with the points we have to make, but we have to answer, or "cross-examine," the points the other side is going to make. We have to support our views with "evidence." We have to "introduce" our subject and come to some "conclusions."

Task 6.1

Brainstorm with a partner until you come up with some interesting controversial issue about which you disagree. It could be a local subject, like parking on campus, or it could be a national or international issue. Then, for five minutes, argue amicably about this issue with your partner. When you are done, discuss with your partner *how* you argued. What did you do? What steps do we take when we try to persuade someone of our views? What do we tend to do first, second, third, and so on when we argue?

Task 6.2

After this one-on-one verbal persuasion, return to your dormitory or apartment or home. Try to write down, in your own voice, your side of the argument, and attempt to persuade your partner of your views. You might now be able to organize your thoughts a little more; you might come up with new points; you might have new answers for her points; you might come across good statistics or examples to help prove your points. At any rate, try writing clearly and persuasively in your own voice. When you are done, look at what you wrote. Analyze it: how does a persuasive written argument work? Does it work any differently from a spoken argument?

Task 6.3

Now, read the following argument by Cicero. This is the longest reading in this book; take your time and work through it carefully. Again it helps to read this out loud—especially since that is surely how Cicero first delivered it. Read as you have read all of the other imitation exercises: noticing not only what Cicero is saying, but how he is saying it. Think about macrostructure and microstructure as you read.[3]

Some background before you read:

Cicero is arguing an interesting case here. It is, really, what would today in the U.S. be a case before the Immigration and Naturalization Service. Cicero is arguing that his client, a poet named Aulus Licinius Archias, is a citizen of Rome, and Cicero is trying to keep Archias from being deported. A law had been passed in 64 B.C. to expel all non-citizens from Rome; it was intended to clear the city of gangs of thugs, not literate, highly esteemed poets. Just as today, when becoming a citizen of the United States confers special rights and privileges, being a citizen of Rome—in an age when the Roman Empire spread over what these people thought of as the known world—was extremely advantageous. Watch how Cicero argues that Archias is a citizen.

But you need to know that the case was not that simple. Archias had become allied with certain political figures in Rome led by Lucius Licinius Lucullus. The other powerful figure in Rome at the time, Pompeius (Pompey), was the political enemy of Lucullus. Clearly the attack on Archias was a way to snipe at Lucullus; if Pompey's followers could get Archias exiled, it would be a nice way to annoy the Lucullus supporters. Dirty politics, perhaps—and Archias was in the middle. If you can think about the way some senators today attack the president's nominees as a way to attack the president, you will understand something of what is occurring in this case.[4] Notice, as you read, how Cicero uses this occasion not just to defend Archias—he gets that part out of the way pretty quickly—but also to score points on other issues.

You are likely to find vocabulary in this translation that is strange to you as you read. Try to discern the meaning of the word from the context, yet do not hesitate to use a dictionary to help you comprehend the passage.[5]

Whatever benefit, gentlemen, can be extracted from any or all of my qualifications, I feel in duty bound to place it at the disposal of Aulus Licinius.[6] I appreciate the limitations of my natural ability. But I cannot deny that my experience as a public speaker has been considerable; and I admit I have never at any time felt a disinclination to study the theoretical background of the art. Upon all my efforts, then, the best I can achieve, Archias has a pre-eminent, overriding claim. For as far as I can cast my mind back into times gone by, as far as I can recollect the earliest years of my boyhood, the picture of the past that takes shape reveals that it was he who first inspired my determination to embark on these studies, and who started me upon their methodical pursuit. And so if this voice of mine, trained by his encouragement and instruction, has on occasion been of service to others, my capacity to come to their assistance—and even to save some of them from destruction—is derived from him: and it is he, therefore, who must receive from me all the help and salvation it lies within my power to provide.

To hear such words from my lips may cause a certain surprise, seeing that his own talents have found expression in spheres far removed from my own study and practice of oratory. But in fact I myself have never concentrated exclusively on this one activity. And besides, all branches of culture are closely related and linked together with one another. A further point, however, which some may equally find surprising, is that in a formal inquiry and official court of justice, at a hearing conducted by a carefully chosen Roman praetor and judges of the highest principles in front of a crowded audience, I have planned that my speech shall assume a form out of keeping with forensic tradition and style. But this deviation from the usual custom happens to be particularly appropriate to my client, yet will not, I hope, cause any inconvenience to yourselves; and so I urge you to allow me this indulgence. The fact is that I am speaking on behalf of an excellent poet, who is also a man of great learning. And I am speaking before listeners of strong literary tastes, judges thoroughly well versed in the humanities, and a praetor of exceptional calibre. What I therefore ask is that you should permit me to enlarge with rather more freedom than usual on cultural and literary matters. The studious seclusion of Archias' life has kept him unacquainted with the hazards of the courts, and it is because of the special nature of his talents that I want to frame my defence in these somewhat novel and unfamiliar terms. If I can but feel that you will have the kindness to concede me this request, I for my part undertake to convince you that Aulus Licinius should not be excluded from the list of Roman citizens; and indeed that he should certainly be made a Roman citizen here and now—if it were not the case that he is one already.

As soon as Archias had grown out of his boyhood and the studies which form a boy's usual liberal training, he began to devote himself to becoming a writer. He came from a good family at Antioch. At that time, it was a city of extensive population and wealth, overflowing with fine scholars and scholarly activities, and it was there that he first succeeded, very rapidly, in showing gifts of an exceptional nature. Later on, when he visited various parts of Asia and toured round the whole of Greece, his arrival in a place would arouse the keenest interest. His talents had by now won him a high reputation, and the excitement aroused by the news of an imminent visit by Archias reached remarkable heights. Nevertheless, even this excited expectation was eclipsed by the admiring enthusiasm with which he was actually received.

Southern Italy was in those days full of Greek culture and learning, and in Latium too such studies were pursued with greater keenness than could be found in the same towns today; while here at Rome also, where the internal situation was peaceful at the time, these pursuits were by no means neglected. Accordingly, Archias was granted citizenship and other honours by Tarentum and Rhegium and Neapolis, and all who were able to recognize a brilliant mind were glad to make his acquaintance and offer him hospitality.

We, too, became aware of his considerable fame, although we had so far never seen him; but soon he made his way to Rome. That was during the consulships of Marius and Catullus, so that the consuls he had the good fortune to find in office included one man who could provide a splendid theme for his pen, and a colleague who was able to supply him not only, again, with notable exploits but also with an appreciative ear. As soon as Archias arrived, while he was still very young, the Lucilli welcomed him to their house—and it is a tribute to his literary genius, and indeed to his whole personality, that the home which was first opened to him in his very youthful years is also the one he most constantly frequents now that he is an older man.

In those early days, Archias also enjoyed the most affectionate relations with the famous Metellus Numidicus and his son Pius. He used to read out his poems to Marcus Aemilius Scaurus. He associated with Quintus Catullus senior and junior. His friendship was cultivated by Lucius Crassus. He was also on very intimate terms not only with the Lucilli but with Drusus and the Octavii and the whole family of Hortensius. He was help in the greatest honour; so much so, indeed, that the roll of his admirers was by no means limited to men who really wanted to learn and listen, but also came to include the sort of people who found it desirable to pretend that they had a taste for such things.

115

Next, after a certain lapse of time, he went to Sicily with Marcus Lucullus, and then, after returning from that province in the company of that gentleman, he proceeded to Heraclea. This was a town which possessed the fullest treaty rights with Rome, and Archias expressed a desire to become a citizen of the place. His own personal qualities were quite sufficient recommendation in themselves, but he also had the support of Lucullus' authority and influence; and his wish was granted by the Heraclean people. In consequence of this, he also received the citizenship of Rome, according to the law of Silvanus and Carbo which granted the franchise to all who have been admitted as citizens of federated towns on the condition that, when the law was passed, the persons concerned were domiciled in Italy. They were also required to report to a praetor within sixty days. Archias had long been resident to Rome, and reported to the praetor Quintus Metellus who was one of his close friends.

If the question of his Roman enfranchisement, and the legal position in this respect, are the only issues we have to bear in mind, I have nothing more to say; and I can close my case. For I am convinced, Gratius, that you would not be able to disprove a single one of these facts. You will not, surely, attempt to deny that he was enrolled at Heraclea at the time of which I am speaking? If this should be your intention, Marcus Lucullus, whose authority and conscience and honour are beyond question, is here to say that he not only believes this happened but also knows it did, that he did not hear of the enrolment from someone else but saw it being done with his own eyes—and indeed, that he was not merely among those present but took the initiative in person. Envoys are also on the spot from Heraclea itself. They are a very distinguished group of men, who have come to Rome specially to attend this case. They are commissioned by their city, they bring with them its official testimonial, and they are prepared to confirm that Archias was, in fact, made a citizen of their town. On this point you have asked for the public archives of Heraclea to be produced; but we all know that they were destroyed when the local record office was burnt during the Italian war. It is ridiculous to ignore proofs which are available, yet to demand evidence which we cannot possibly obtain; to be deliberately silent about things that men are actually in a position to remember, but to clamour for documentary record. You have the word of a great and scrupulous gentleman. You have the sworn affidavit of an irreproachably honest town council. There can be no tampering with things like that. Yet you brush them aside and call for documents! And you do this although you admit in the same breath that the possibility that such records might be forged is seen by experience to be considerable.

Or do you propose to deny that Archias lived at Rome? Surely not! Years before he ever became a Roman citizen he had established Rome as his residence, and the place where all his wordly possessions were concentrated. Or did he omit to report? No, he reported as he should have. Indeed, out of all the registrations sought from the board of praetors at the time, his was actually the only application which was accompanied by truly valid supporting evidence.

There were allegations that the citizen-lists of Appius had not been very carefully kept. Indeed, the authenticity of all such compilations had been cast into doubt first by the unreliability of Gabinius, before he was condemned by the court, and then by the discredit brought upon him by his conviction. Nevertheless the conscientious and law-abiding Metellus Pius exhibited such scruples with regard to these lists that he went to the praetor Lucius Lentulus and a board of judges, and indicated to them that he was extremely disturbed at having to erase even one single name. And yet when you consider the documents which related to the present case, you will see that there is not the slightest question of any erasure in respect of the name of Aulus Licinius.

These facts regarding his position at Rome are very far from suggesting any doubts about his previous enfranchisement at Heraclea. Besides, as to that, Heraclea was by no means the only town where he came a citizen. It has, as a matter of fact, been not uncommon for the Greek communities of Italy to bestow their citizenship for no particular reason at all, even on individuals whose qualifications were extremely slender or non-existent. So how can you venture to suggest that the people of Rhegium, Locri, Neapolis, or Tarentum, when they were perfectly prepared to make a habit of bestowing such honours even upon mere actors, would have refused it to this man of really brilliant and outstanding gifts?

All the other persons whose Roman status has been questioned contrived to insinuate their names into the citizen-lists of their municipalities not merely after the dates of their alleged enrolment but even after the passing of the Papian law. But my client, on the other hand, does not even think it necessary to cite the lists on which his name was inscribed, because there has never been a time during all this period at which he has not looked upon himself as belonging to Heraclea. You say you miss his name on the census-rolls. But is it really such a deadly secret that at the time of the last census he was with the army, on the staff of the eminent Lucius Lucullus, and on the immediately preceding occasion he was likewise with Lucullus, during the latter's quaestorship in Asia? The census before that, when Julius and Crassus were censors—the first after his enfranchisement—is irrelevant since on that occasion no registration of any part of the population was in fact conducted at all.

In any case, however, it has to be recognized that census lists are no real proof of Roman citizenship, but merely indicate that the men whose names appear on them claimed it at that particular time. It may therefore be helpful for me to add that during the years in question my client, so far from not being one of our citizens even in his own eyes (as you pretended), made his will on a number of occasions according to Roman law, received legacies left him by Roman citizens, and was recommended to the treasury by the proconsul Lucius Lucullus, as Roman, so that a reward might be given him for his services.

As regards your contrary assertions, the burden of proving them rests with you and no one but you. For no judgements he has passed on himself, and no judgements passed on him by his friends, will be of the smallest assistance towards the refutation of his claim.

You will no doubt be asking me, Gratius, why I feel such an affection for this man. The answer is that he provides my mind with refreshment after this din of the courts; he soothes my ears to rest when they are wearied by angry disputes. How could I find material, do you suppose, for the speeches I make every day on such a variety of subjects, unless I steeped my mind in learning? How could I endure the constant strains if I could not distract myself from them by this means? Yes, I confess I am devoted to the study of literature. If people have buried themselves in books, if they have used nothing they have read for the benefit of their fellow-men, if they have never displayed the fruits of such reading before the public eye, well, let them by all means be ashamed of the occupation. But why, gentlemen, would I feel any shame? Seeing that not once through all these years have I allowed myself to be prevented from helping any man in the hour of his need because I wanted a rest, or because I was eager to pursue my own pleasures, or even because I needed a sleep!

I cannot therefore, I submit, be justly rebuked or censured if the time which others spend in advancing their own personal affairs, taking holidays and attending Games, indulging in pleasures of various kinds or even enjoying mental relaxation and bodily recreation, the time they spend on protracted parties and gambling and playing ball, proves in my case to have been taken up with returning over and over again to these literary pursuits. And I have all the more right to engage in such studies because they improve my capacity as a speaker; and this, for what it is worth, has unfailingly remained at the disposal of my friends whenever prosecutions have placed them in danger. Even if some may regard my ability as nothing very great, at least I realize the source from which the best part of it has come. For unless I had convinced myself from my earliest years, on the basis of lessons derived from all I had read, that nothing in life is really worth having except moral decency and reputable behavior, and that for their sake all physical tortures and all perils of death and banishment must be held of little account, I should never have been able to speak up for the safety of you all in so many arduous clashes, or to endure these attacks which dissolute rogues launch against me every day. The whole of literature, philosophy and history is full of examples which teach this lesson—but which would have been plunged in utter darkness if the written word had not been available to illuminate them. Just think of the number of vividly drawn pictures of valiant men of the past that Greek and Latin writers have preserved for our benefit: not for mere inspection only, but for imitation as well. Throughout my public activities I have never ceased to keep these great figures before my eyes, and have modeled myself heart and soul on the contemplation of their excellence.

It might be objected that those great men, whose noble deeds have been handed down in the literary record, were not themselves by any means thoroughly well versed in the learning which I praise too highly. Certainly, it would be difficult to make a categorical assertion that they were. Nevertheless, I am quite clear what my answer to such a point should be. I agree that there have been many people whose exceptional inborn qualities, expressed in almost godlike endowments of mind and character without the support of any cultural qualifications at all, have enabled them by their own unaided endeavors to reach the heights of self-management and moral excellence. Indeed, I would go further, and express the view that the number of virtuous and admirable men produced by character without learning exceeds those who are the products of learning without character. Nevertheless I do also maintain that, when noble and elevated natural gifts are supplemented and shaped by the influence of theoretical knowledge, the result is then something truly remarkable and unique. Such a personality could be seen by our fathers in the superhuman figure of the younger Scipio Africanus. Such, too, were those paragons of moderation and self-control Gaius Laelius and Lucius Furius; such was the courageous and venerable Marcus Cato, the most erudite man of his day. They would certainly never have spent their time on literary studies if these had not helped them to understand what a better life could be, and how to bring that ideal into effect for themselves.

And yet let us leave aside for a moment any practical advantage that literary studies may bring. For even if their aim were pure enjoyment and nothing else, you would still, I am sure, feel obliged to agree that no other activity of the mind could possibly have such a broadening and enlightening effect. For there is no other occupation upon earth which is so appropriate to every time and every age and every place. Reading stimulates the young and diverts the old, increases one's satisfaction when things are going well, and when they are going badly provides refuge and solace. It is a delight in the home; it can be fitted in with public life; throughout the night, on journeys, in the country, it is a companion which never lets me down.

And indeed even if we ourselves were not capable of any inclination or taste for these pursuits, we ought all the same to feel admiration when we see such gifts exemplified in others. No one can have been so boorish and insensitive that he remained unaffected when Roscius recently died. Although he was an old man at the time of his death, we had a feeling that such a superb and attractive artist ought somehow to have been exempted from our common fate. And if such a man's mere physical comportment on the stage was enough to win the hearts of us all, surely we cannot be left indifferent by genius of a purely intellectual kind, with all its enigmatic motions and scintillations.

Many is the time, gentlemen, that I have listened to this Archias—for I am going to presume on your indulgence, since I see that the unconventional shape of my speech has succeeded in gaining your attention—many is the time I have listened to him improvising qualities of admirable verses about topics of the day without having written down one single letter before he spoke. Many times also I have heard him respond to demands for an encore by repeating the same subject-matter in an entirely new set of words and phrases. And as for his written works, the products of meticulous care and cogitation, I have seen them accorded a degree of appreciation in no way inferior to the reverence felt for writers of ancient times. Should I not love and admire such a man, and deem it my duty to defend him by every means in my power?

We have it on eminent and learned authority that, whereas other arts need to be based upon study and rules and principles, poets depend entirely on their own inborn gifts and are stimulated by some internal force, a sort of divine spark, within the depths of their own souls. Our great Ennius was therefore right to call poets holy, because they seem to bring to us some special gift and endowment which the gods have accorded them as a passport for this world. Even the most barbarous of races has never treated the name of poet with disrespect. How imperative therefore it is that you yourselves, with all your noble culture, should regard it as holy indeed! The very rocks and deserts echo the poet's song. Many is the time when ferocious beasts have been enchanted and arrested in their tracks as these strains come to their ears. Shall we, then, who have been nurtured on everything that is fine, remain unmoved at a poet's voice?

The people of Colophon declare that Homer came from their city, the Chians assert he belongs to them, the men of Salamis lay a rival claim, while the people of Smyrna are so sure he is theirs that they have even allotted him a shrine within their town; and a great many other communities, too, have joined in this competitive struggle to be regarded as Homer's birth-place. These people, in fact, are eager for the possession of a man who has long been dead and who, even when he lived, was a foreigner. It is because of his poetic genius that they feel this powerful urge. Are we, on the contrary, to reject a poet who is still alive, and who is indeed ours by law, and ours by his own inclination as well?

This would be particularly misguided in the case of Archias, since he has for many years past devoted all his expert skill and talent to celebrating the glorious renown of

Rome. When he was a young man he wrote about the Cimbrian war, and he even succeeded in gaining the approval of Gaius Marius himself, although that great man did not have a reputation for appreciating this kind of activity. But no one is, in fact, so uninterested in the Muses that he does not want his own deeds to be glorified and perpetuated in verse. There is a story that the renowned Athenian Themistocles was asked which actor or singer he liked the best. His favourite, he replied, was whichever one praised his exploits the most highly! And that, for example, was the reason why Gaius Marius was attached to Lucius Plotius, whose gifts he saw to be well fitted for the commemoration of the deeds that he himself had accomplished.

Archias has also dealt with the entire war against Mithridates, a vast and complicated war consisting of many varied operations on land and sea. This work sheds lustre on the valiant and magnificent Lucius Lucullus, but in so doing it contributes to the splendour of Rome as well. For it was Romans whom Lucullus led to open up Pontus, protected though it was by the resources of its king and by its own geographical position. It was Romans who under the same general, with a force of only moderate size, put the numberless hordes of Armenians to flight. It was Romans, still under the direction of Lucullus, who gained the glory for rescuing and preserving the friendly city of Cyzicus from all the onslaughts of the king and the ravening jaws of warfare. To Rome, too, comes eternal honour for that amazing naval battle at Tenedos in which Lucullus slew the enemy's admirals and crushed their fleet. Ours are the trophies, ours the monuments, ours the triumphs. Those who dedicate their powers to the literary celebration of such events are increasing the fame of the people of Rome itself.

Our noble Ennius was held in affection by the elder Africanus, and the tomb of the Scipios is said to have contained a marble statue of the poet. And yet his compliments to Africanus surely illuminate not only that hero himself but the entire commonwealth of Rome. Ennius also extolled to the skies the Cato whose great-grandson is with us today; and bright is the brilliance shed by those panegyrics upon the renown of our country in general. In the same way, again, when compliments are paid to the names of Maximus, Marcellus and Fulvius, it is all of us Romans, and not just themselves, to whom distinction is added by such eulogies. That is why the writer from Rudiae who uttered these praises was admitted by our ancestors to the citizenship of Rome.

The man whom we are now considering possesses the franchise of Heraclea. Many other Greek townships, too, have competed to make him a citizen of their own communities. He has also received a similar gift, by due legal process from Rome itself. How on earth can we deprive him of this manifest entitlement?

Archias is a Greek poet. But it would be entirely wrong to suppose that Greek poetry ranks lower than Latin in value. For Greek literature is read in almost every country in the world, whereas Latin is understood only within its own boundaries which, as you must admit, are restricted. Our deeds, it is true, extend to all the regions of the earth. But the effect of this should be to inspire us with the determination that every country where the strong arm of Rome has carried its weapons should also be given an opportunity to learn of our illustrious achievements. For literary commemoration is a most potent factor in enhancing a country's prestige. And to those who hazard their lives for the sake of glory, such literature is a vigorous incentive, stimulating them to risk fearful perils and perform noble endeavours.

We are told that Alexander the Great took around with him a great number of authors engaged in writing about his achievements. And yet, as he stood beside the tomb of Achilles at Sigeum, he uttered these words: "Fortunate youth, who found Homer to proclaim your valour!" He was right; for, if the *Iliad* had never existed, the tomb where Achilles' body was buried would have buried his memory as well. And then again Pompeius known as Magnus, outstanding alike for his bravery and good fortune, conferred Roman citizenship upon Theophanes of Mitylene, the history of his deeds, before his whole assembled army. Now, our gallant men, countryfolk and soldiers though they were, felt influenced by the splendid tale Theophanes had told. And so, feeling that part of the grandeur belonged also to themselves, they declared their approval with a mighty shout.

If the law did not happen to have made Archias a Roman citizen already, he would find it the easiest thing in the world, as I am certain you cannot deny, to win the franchise from one of our generals in this selfsame way. Surely Sulla, who dispensed citizenship so freely to Spaniards and Gauls, would never have refused such a request from Archias. Once, at a public meeting, some bad poet from out of the crowd handed Sulla an epigram the man had written about him, with every other line longer than it ought to be. Sulla, who was conducting an auction, immediately ordered a reward to be paid the scribbler from its proceeds—on the condition that he never wrote anything again! Here then was a personage who felt that even the worst of poets should be rewarded for his industry; so how could he have failed to help a writer with the talent and style and fluency of Archias? Or, again, if Quintus Metellus Pius had been approached, the personal influence of Archias, not to speak of the intervention of the Luculli, would unmistakably have been successful, especially as Metellus was his intimate friend and had, besides, conferred the franchise on numerous other people as well. Moreover, Metellus was eager to have his own actions recorded; he even gave a hearing to certain poets who came from Corduba, for all the ponderous, exotic flavour of their language.

For there is no concealing the fact, and it had better be accepted and openly admitted: we all like to be praised! The better the man the greater his desire for celebrity. The philosophers who bid us despise ambition do not forget to affix their names to their own books! On the very writings in which they deplore publicity and self-advertisement, they publicize and advertise themselves. And then again that heroic commander Decimus Brutus, when he erected temples and monuments, adorned their forecourts with verses written by his friend Accius. Another outstanding example is

Fulvius, who took Ennius with him on his campaign against the Aetolians, and when it was over forthwith dedicated the spoils of war to the Muses. In a city, then, where even generals scarcely lay down their weapons before offering honours to poetry and the Muses' shrine, it would indeed be unbecoming for judges, who wear the garb of peace, to act in a fashion repugnant to the honour of those divinities and the well-being of the poetical profession.

To incline you to my way of thinking, gentlemen, I will place myself in your hands and confess to you my own passion to be famous. This is a passion which may seem exaggerated; but I am sure it is not dishonourable. The fact is that the measures which I took during my consulship, with your collaboration, to ensure the salvation of this city and the empire and the lives of all its citizens and everything that our country stands for, have been chosen by Archias as the subject of a poem. He has already started upon its composition, and when he read out to me what he had written, I judged the project a very worthwhile and attractive one, and singled him out as just the man for the task.

A person with right ideas hopes for no reward whatever for any toils and perils he may have to undergo—except only praise, and the good opinion of his fellows. Take those things away, gentlemen, and in the brief and transient span of this life I cannot see what stimulus remains to encourage our arduous labours. If the human spirit felt no anticipations of posterity, if the range of its imagination were bounded by the limits that circumscribe human existence, we should never be prepared to tire ourselves out with all these exertions, suffer torments of sleepless anxiety, face ceaseless confrontations in which our very lives are at stake. It does appear, however, that men of true nobility contain within themselves a force which day and night applies the prick of ambition to their hearts, and never allows us to stop struggling to ensure that the memory of our names shall not perish with our deaths, but shall survive them for all time to come.

For how could we, who undergo the toils and hazards of public life, be spiritless enough to feel satisfied with the idea that, after we have spent not one single moment of our lives in peace and tranquility, all this effort will go for nothing at the very moment when we die? Many distinguished men have taken great pains to leave their statues and representations behind them. But those are likenesses only of the body, and not of the spirit at all, and so have not we all the more reason to feel enthusiastic about bequeathing a similar image of our intellectual and moral personalities as well, to be molded and elaborated by the very finest talents available?

As for myself, even at the actual time when I was busiest with great matters, I felt I was also diffusing and disseminating a knowledge of those very same deeds throughout the entire earth to be remembered for ever. Perhaps, when I am dead, I shall no longer be able to perceive whether their memory does, in fact, remain. Or possibly, as certain philosophers have argued, some part of my being will still be conscious that this is happening. But however that may be, at least I derive satisfaction here and now from the thought and the hope that what I have done will not be forgotten.

So I call upon you, judges, to pronounce in favour of my client. He is a man whose honourable character you see confirmed by the high rank of his friends and the unbroken durations of their friendships with him. You can appreciate his gifts from the extent to which they have been in demand from leading men who are extremely gifted themselves. Moreover, the justice of his cause is demonstrated by the sanction of the law, the authority of his municipality, the testimony offered by Lucullus, and archives going back to Metellus.

To you and your generals and the deeds of the Roman people Archias has always done honour. To those recent internal perils which threatened myself and yourselves he proposes to offer an undying testimonial of praise. He belongs, moreover, to a profession which has universally and at all times been declared and believed to possess a sacred character. If then, gentlemen, such great powers warrant the applause of mankind—and truly they deserve the commendation of the gods themselves!—I entreat you to take him under your protection. Let it not be said that a severe judgement of yours has done harm to such a man. Let it be seen instead that your humane decision has brought him relief.

I have made the statement of my case as brief and simple as usual; and I have the feeling that it has gained your approbation. I hope my digression from the custom of the courts and the bar, in order to tell you something about my client's talent and about literary studies in general, has been to your taste. To the chairman of this tribunal—I venture to express the conviction—it has proved acceptable enough.

Task 6.4

Now, try to write your own Ciceronian oration (or, if you like, "argument").

> First, brainstorm some topics you might argue about. It might help to stay close to the form of the law courts—you might imagine defending a fellow student on some traffic violation, or a charge before the university disciplinary committee. But you can range further if you like—you might wish to take on a serious political topic. You can take the "proof" you wrote in the previous chapter on Thomas Aquinas and revise it into a Ciceronian oration.
>
> Then try to produce your own argument in the voice of Cicero. Go back and think about what macrostructures shape the whole speech; then look at his individual sentences and see what diction and syntax create the voice of Cicero. Start small; remember, this is only a draft.[7]

Bring your imitation to class and discuss it with two partners. Laugh, if you like, about what you wrote; note sentences and phrases that mimic Cicero's well. See who got the closest to his macrostructure and some of his microstructures. Does your argument persuade your partners? Did their arguments persuade you? Why or why not? Did you not answer all of their counterarguments? Do you not have enough evidence for some of your points?

Here is a student's attempt at imitating a Ciceronian argument. Krista Raef takes a serious subject and treats it in the serious tone of the Ciceronian oration. She has recently read both the *Odyssey*, Homer's tale of the clever, wily Greek who spends ten years trying to get home after the Trojan War, and the *Aeneid*, the Roman poet Virgil's tale of one of the few Trojans to survive the wreckage of Troy who then, after many trials, moves to Italy with his men and founds Rome. Working out of the previous chapter, she has framed a question—which of these two is the better leader?—and then cast her answer (her *thesis*) in the form of a Ciceronian oration, attempting to persuade her audience of the truth of her thesis.[8]

Aeneas' Leadership

When contemplating leadership in today's world, I feel obligated to look to Virgil and his literary epic, The Aeneid. In my years of study in this renowned place, I have come to realize the significance of taking one's knowledge and applying it to life. I do have limitations; others are more intelligent than I when it comes to the knowledge available in literature. But I have studied for three years here, and will be concluding this chapter in my life and making my exodus and mark on the world in the very near future, and that cannot be ignored. Thus, it is worthy to listen to my claim, for you yourselves, most intelligent readers of classical literature, can make your time in this place more fruitful and advantageous if you begin to look to the wisdom of the great works that we read.

My words may surprise you, for my own profound study is in another field. Yet, never have I limited myself to studying just one field; it is vital that we study our liberal education so as to acquire a great expanse of knowledge, which comes from all fields and not just one. With that said, I believe it is imperative that we look to Aeneas, the hero of

Virgil's literary epic, for the qualities of leadership that we ought to have within whenever we leave this haven and pursue our purposes in this world. It is Aeneas that enables me to understand better the nature of a leader, especially in our great and democratic nation. And so I attempt to teach to others that which I have been taught from Virgil's Aeneas. I undertake to persuade you that the Virgilian sense of a hero, evident in the remarkable leadership of Aeneas, is the true example of a good leader throughout the epic, especially when compared to the Homeric hero, displayed in the clever Odysseus, even after consideration of the differing aims of the two heroes.

Throughout Virgil's epic, Aeneas exhibits certain qualities of a good leader, especially in Book IV. It is clear that a leader must be selfless, placing the good of his people above his own natural desires and inclinations. In this book, Dido, the founder and queen of Carthage, falls in love with Aeneas, and it is suggested that the two take part in a wedding ceremony. Aeneas remains in Carthage at Dido's side, "laying foundations for new towers and homes" (354). He is quite content to aid Dido with her city, building new additions to her town and staying with his one love. Yet, after Mercury delivers to Aeneas the message that Jove desires him to hear, Aeneas responds to the "command / From heaven" (382–83), immediately deliberating all possible actions. When arriving on a conclusion, Aeneas orders his men to prepare the ships for sea in a silent and secretive manner, deciding to follow the implication given by Jove. When confronted by the queen, Aeneas tells her, "first of all / I should look after Troy and the loved relics / Left me of my people," ranking the concern and benefit of his people above the feelings in his heart (471–73). In this way, Aeneas gives the people's good its proper precedence over the "emotion in his heart," selflessly sacrificing his own wants in order to lead his people to the land of Italy as he is supposed to (457).

Next, Aeneas demonstrates another quality of a good leader in this same episode, the quality of arranging reason and will over his passions. After he speaks with Dido, who is clearly very upset and furious with Aeneas, the queen hurries from his sight; and the question is not whether Aeneas cares for her, but what action he chooses. At this very moment, Aeneas is left standing there, "shaken still / With love of her" (IV, 549–50). There is no denying that love is a passion. Then, instead of pursuing that love and following the fervor of his heart, the great leader chooses to go "back to the fleet" (551). It is "then with a will" that Aeneas sends off his ships (551). He puts his will, the determination that his people must have their city, above the passionate feelings for the queen, observing his strength of mind and purpose.

If the investigation of Aeneas regarding the qualities of good leadership is the only concern we have, then my argument is finished and I can offer no more. Such facts are obvious, and I believe you would not negate any of them. Surely you will not deny that Aeneas placed his own desires underneath the good of the people? If you attempt to make such a claim, it should be known that King Iarbus, a previous suitor to the queen of Carthage, is here to give testimony against such insinuations, informing us of how he heard by rumor about the marriage of Aeneas and Dido. He can gladly testify what he has come to know:

> How this Aeneas landed, Trojan born,
> How Dido in her beauty graced his company,
> Then how they reveled all the winter long
> Unmindful of the realm, prisoners of lust. (262–65)

It is this passion that Dido and Aeneas show in remaining together in their loving place that proves Aeneas' desires.

Do you propose that the characteristic of selflessness was evident in the Homeric hero, Odysseus? Absolutely not! Odysseus loses his people gradually, so that by the time he reaches his homeland, he is the sole survivor. This proves that Odysseus put his own desire, that of returning to his kingdom, above the good of his men, for if he were considering the benefit of his people, he would have realized that they, too, wanted to return home; he would have made an attempt to condemn their recklessness and head home without being so curious and willing to explore. Throughout the poem, Homer delves into and emphasizes the *oikos*, or the community, yet Odysseus returns to his homeland without a single member of his community of men.

Doubtless you will be wondering about the differing aims of the two heroes. This must be taken into account, for it could influence what is meant by calling a man a good leader, which is what we are being shown through Aeneas. How could I begin comparison of the heroes of Homer and Virgil without considering the goals of each leader of men? Yes, I acknowledge that both men had distinct intentions and such a difference could easily explain the inconsistency in the two roles of leadership. Indeed, I propound that Homer's hero, Odysseus, has the goal of returning to his homeland after several long years of wandering and drifting from place to place, while remaining in some places longer than others. Conversely, Virgil's hero, Aeneas, has the intent of founding a new city in a foreign land, following the duty into which he was born.

How do I explain, then, the differences in leadership between the two? I believe that Odysseus, Homer's hero, is an example of perseverance and wit in face of the unceasing obstacles of life. However, I think that Virgil's hero, Aeneas, is an active illustration of a great and pious leader, one who employs reason and is "duty-bound" to found and establish a new homeland for his Roman people (545). We do believe, after all, in the good and benefit of the people in this democracy of our nation, do we not?

I summon you, intelligent readers of literature, to reason over what I have put forth about Aeneas. Call to mind and allow yourselves to appreciate his great qualities and talents that, as a leader, only Virgil's Aeneas has truly reached. We can see how honorable he is in leading his men selflessly and rationally to a foreign land, arriving with large numbers of them so that he can properly establish his new city. We can also note his strength of mind, which allows him to make intelligent decisions with reasoning, instead of letting his passions rule his decision making.

In investigating this manner more deeply, I hope it is clear how we have benefited from Aeneas and his leadership. He is but one man, yet he is the sole founder of a new kingdom and a new identity, not for himself and his selfish desires but for the good of his own people. Thinking back on Odysseus, we see a man who is struggling to return home, for home is a large part of his identity from which he cannot part if he desires to keep and preserve his destiny.

Keep in mind that this epic, like those of Homer, strives to portray a very real picture of life. We can, indeed, learn from Virgil's epic, for in the fighting of the second portion of the epic, we can comprehend the battle is not worth fighting unless we know for what it is we are fighting. In this case the fight is for the founding of a new identity, one based on leading the "whole world under law's dominion" (IV, 315). Such an epic speaks to us and to the larger audience throughout time, hinting that law is upstanding and respectable; were it not for Virgil's Aeneas, it is quite possible that we could not comprehend the importance of law in today's world. This law of the people is just as essential in today's time as it was in the time of Virgil and his Aeneas.

I have stated that which I set out to proclaim, and I have the impression that your consent is forthcoming. If then we are to rely on such literary works in order to gain deeper understanding of our own world and meaning of life in today's time, I implore you to take heed of all that Virgil's Aeneas has done, especially in a time when good leaders are quite needed. Do not let it be understood that you, bright readers of literature, have failed to learn great things from this man. Instead, let it be known that you have observed the selflessness and reasoning that is so evident in this great leader and will, indeed, seek such good leaders among yourselves.

Great Ideas: Rhetoric and
the Seven Liberal Arts

If you are using this book in a college or university composition class, you may be working in some division of the school called The College of Liberal Arts and Sciences or some similar name. The concept of the "liberal arts" has a fascinating history, and rhetoric's place in the liberal arts has been a vexed one.

The idea of the "liberal arts" has its roots in ancient Greece. "Liberal" here does not mean the politics of the political left, and "arts" does not merely mean the "fine arts," painting and music and sculpture. *Ars* is the Latin translation of the Greek word *techne*, from which we get the words technology and technique. It is closer to our words "skill" or "competency." Most arts were practical arts, like blacksmithing, cobbling (making shoes), and making wine. These were the "servile" arts. And "liberal" means free, so the liberal arts were/are the arts of "free men," that is, those who had the time and leisure (provided them by their economic situation and slaves) to think about the arts that did not accomplish anything directly practical: philosophy, ethics, writing, and so on. But there was also a strain of thought that said that these were the arts that *made* you "liberal," free: by thinking philosophically, you free your mind from the prison house of the merely practical, and more importantly from your own biases and prejudices and parochial attitudes, so that you begin to see the truth of things.

Now, which were the liberal arts? What should a person study if he wanted to be one of these types of "liberal" men? It is not an idle question; the question here is, What should be the curriculum for any school that seeks to produce free men? (A related form of this question is, Why does almost every college and university in the United States require you to take composition in some form? I will discuss that question below.) There was some flux over the years, but several "arts" remained consistent. By the Middle Ages, the curriculum was charted out in a fairly standard way and described fully. In the eleventh century, when every cathedral was required to have a school, the masters at the cathedral school of Chartres shaped them into seven liberal arts (seven being an important number in Christian medieval Europe), to be studied in this order: grammar, dialectic (what we would call logic), rhetoric, arithmetic, geometry, astronomy, music. You will see that the first three of the subjects are about language; together they were called the trivium (*tri* = three; *via* = way or road)—the three-fold initial way to truth. You studied languages (including not just what we would call "grammar," but poetry and literary criticism), logic (that is, how to use language to discover truth), and rhetoric (how to use language to persuade others of the truth). The next four subjects are about numbers and were called the quadrivium (*quad* = four); one studied arithmetic (numbers in themselves), geometry (numbers in three dimensions, that is, shapes), astronomy (those shapes as perfect spheres up in the sky), and music (in this case, the "music of the spheres"—that perfect sound that the planets make when they rotate in their perfectly spherical orbits). The ultimate goal of this curriculum was to prepare you to study theology, the queen of the sciences.

There was a dispute about the order of dialectic and rhetoric. Most said that logic came first—you had to discover truth before you could persuade others of it. But some—especially philosophers and professional logicians—argued that logic was a "higher" art than rhetoric. Logic is about truth, they would say; rhetoric is just about using language to manipulate people into agreeing with you by using emotion and verbal fireworks. Rhetoric was therefore just barely above—gasp!—literature, which we all know is not about truth at all, but fiction, lies!

The dispute appears in several fascinating texts in the Western tradition. Socrates, in Plato's dialogues, rails against the "Sophists"; these were the teachers of rhetoric in ancient Greece. Socrates thought that these Sophists were not interested in pursuing truth, but just in teaching people how to get ahead in life, how to manipulate others with language. We still use the term "sophistry" today to mean this, largely because Plato won the argument—in large part through his brilliant rhetorical move of using fictionalized dialogues to make his points. Cicero, in Rome, revived rhetoric's respect for a time; he saw that in the process of invention one was indeed discovering the truth of what one had to say, and in formulating one's argument, one had to do more than just manipulate—one had to persuade, with true evidence, towards the truth.

In the years before Rome fell to the invading Vandal tribes, a young teacher of rhetoric, Augustine, was living in Carthage and becoming quite a success. By this time, in many circles rhetoric had degraded from Cicero's idea to being more or less a matter of correctness, or worse, of fancy techniques; to study rhetoric, you studied and applied these clever verbal techniques. In his book *Confessions*, a sort of spiritual autobiography, Augustine tells how he found this life ultimately empty. He discovers philosophy (not coincidentally by reading Cicero's treatise *Hortensius*), that is, the desire for truth and wisdom, and not just clever wordplay, and decides to quit his life as a teacher of rhetoric. Gradually he moves toward the Christian church, but one thing that holds him back is that, by the standards of the rhetoric he was taught, the Bible is so poorly written that he cannot believe it holds any truth to it. Ultimately, he does convert—crucially, it is *reading* that is the catalyst—and goes on to become perhaps the greatest theologian—and one of the greatest rhetoricians—the Christian faith has ever had. In a later book, *De doctrina christiana* (*On Christian Doctrine*), he formulated a Christian notion of rhetoric that would explain how the writing in the Bible is in fact good writing—and in the process he restructured education on a new model. This laid the basis for rhetoric's revival during the Middle Ages, when it again contended with dialectic as a legitimate art.

During the Renaissance and Early Modern period, however, rhetoric again becomes a vexed question. A French thinker, Peter Ramus, again severed invention and organization from rhetoric; he said that the getting of a topic and the organizing of what one had to say were the skills of logic, and rhetoric was just the study of how to "ornament," to "dress up" what one had to say in fancy thoughts. Once more, rhetoric was merely the prettifying of one's thoughts, and you see in many writers of the time—not least of them, Shakespeare—a constant worrying about whether one is expressing truth or just manipulating, using "plain speech" or hiding the truth in "figures" or "metaphors." Add to this the fact that the new scientific thinking was coming along to require plain, direct explanations of observed phenomena, and rhetoric suffered a further blow to its reputation.

This dispute continues today. You can find people in some philosophy departments (the child of the dialectic faculty of the medieval university) who feel that they practice a higher, more important art than those in the English department—and especially a higher art than those who teach lowly composition courses. Scientists have been known to express the same kind of prejudice—that they really discover what is "true" about the world while those in the "liberal arts" areas are just playing with words. Of course, one thing that gives the lie to this conceit is that scientists are constantly resorting to metaphors (the "Big Bang," the "double helix," "quarks," "messenger RNA") to express their concepts and discoveries. And clearly most schools still think rhetoric is a crucial art, or they would not require English and composition departments to put every student through one or two semesters of composition. Scholars study different modes of rhetoric, how real writers write, how best to teach students how to write, how students should be graded on their writing, and much more. In fact, this book grew out of my teaching many composition courses crossing with my interest in rhetoric in the Middle Ages.

There are even two textbooks that use Cicero's principles to teach composition and which are quite well known in the field: Edward P. J. Corbett's *Classical Rhetoric for the Modern Student* and Winifred Bryan Horner's *Rhetoric in the Classical Tradition*. If you want to learn more about classical rhetoric, you could do worse than to start with these two books—or with Cicero himself, whose works are available in many popular translations.

Task 6.5

Based on your reading, discussion, and workshops, revise your Ciceronian oration. Try to get the microstructure and macrostructure as close as you can to the original.

Task 6.6

Write in your journal about this experience. How was writing the Ciceronian imitation different from arguing in your "own" voice? How did changing the voice and style change what you said and how you said it? What else did you learn from this exercise? As we near the end of this book, what have you learned about writing?

Why We're Doing This

So much of the persuasive writing that we still use today is fundamentally in Ciceronian form—in speeches, business memos, editorials and columns in newspapers. This is simply one of the fundamental macrostructures that all educated women and men must know, be able to analyze, and be able to produce themselves if they are going to be successful in the world of discourse. If you can understand, become competent in, and even master this form, you will be able to read complex arguments and see where they are going, and be able to respond to them. More immediately, when they assign a paper, most professors expect you to turn in writing that is in some way or another structured according to this form. So, learn this macrostructure and I can almost guarantee that it will increase your success with written and spoken material.

Furthermore, if you can work your way through the complex microstructures that make up the Ciceronian voice, you will be able to comprehend almost any complex writing you will come up against. And if you can reproduce with your own words these complex microstructures, people will begin to use words like "eloquent" and "graceful" when they describe your prose. In short, the Ciceronian voice is a ticket to success in any endeavor where words and argumentation are predominant. So we are doing this to give you a chance to be successful.

But it is also just wonderful in its own right. When you can see and produce for yourself the elegant lines of a Ciceronian discourse, you are joining a select group of people who can appreciate the beauties of a very refined use of language. Enjoy it.

Extra Exercises for Those Who Want to Do More

*Analyze a business memo, newspaper editorial, or maga-
zine article, finding the parts of a Ciceronian oration. See
if you can find the* exordium, *the* partitio, *the* narratio, refutatio, *et cetera. How does the writer play with this macrostructure, switching the order of parts, cutting some
and expanding others? What does this tell you about the
writer's purpose, the audience she is writing to, or the
voice in which it is written?*

*Listen to a speech and do the same as above. Can you
catch these parts on the fly, with your ear? If so, you are
beginning to internalize these parts of a Ciceronian oration quite well.*

*If one of your classes has an electronic component (email,
bulletin board, chat, etc.), "argue" a topic related to the
class on the electronic discussion, and then restructure
your position in a second post that lays out your views
in coherent Ciceronian form. Try to achieve not just the
macrostructure but also the microstructures of Cicero's
voice in your second post.*

*Write a guest opinion piece for your school newspaper
on some current topic that is important to you. Use what
you have learned from Cicero to help you mold your writing. The ego boost from seeing your words in print can be
a great incentive to learning more about argumentative
writing.*

*Read Jonathan Swift's "A Modest Proposal." This satirical
piece, written in Ireland in the eighteenth century, argues
that the way to remedy the horrible conditions of poverty
is to . . . well, I will let you discover that for yourself.
Now that you have imitated Cicero, you will also see quite
clearly that Swift imitates and parodies the Ciceronian*

oration with astonishing care and maintains a deadpan tone throughout; the humor, and the political effectiveness, in many ways rely on the audience knowing the conventions of a Ciceronian argument. Enjoy the reading, then produce your own "Modest Proposal" for solving a contemporary problem.

Chapter Seven

Voices of Negotiation: Shaping Your World

*I*f you have assiduously worked, explored, practiced, and imitated your way through this book, by now you have developed a much larger set of writing skills. You know how to start from "nothing" and develop it into "something." You know how to take that "something" and give shape and order to it, and by now are well on your way to being able to craft your "something" in intelligent and even elegant ways. Through imitating others' voices, you have developed not only skills like description and argumentation, but also a set of models and masters who can always shape your writing. Furthermore, you should have learned by now that one of the best ways to learn more about writing, and expand your own abilities, is to find more masters, more models, and then learn from them by imitating them.

You began as an apprentice. It is a long process, this apprenticeship. In most trades it lasts six or seven years before you create your "masterpiece"—again, the *first* piece of work that will qualify you to be a "master" and not just an apprentice.

Now let us end with one more set of exercises, one last imitating of the masters. It combines many of the skills you have been learning over the course of this book's chapters. We began our process of learning to write by imitation with a deceptively simple exercise: describing a person. We end with another exercise that may seem simple: writing a letter. In this day of inexpensive long-distance telephone rates, people do not write personal letters as often as they used to do, but in fact, letters and memoranda are still a crucial means of communication in the public world of business and the professions. In the business world people write letters to each other all the time for different reasons: to request information, to give instructions, to protest an action, to lay out plans for the future. And in your private life you probably have also written at least a few letters: thank-you notes for presents you received, letters to people (grandparents?) far away, and yes, even love letters expressing your feelings for someone. Today, email has replaced much letter writing, but it is essentially the same thing and used often for the same purposes—a communication from one person to the next, though, as befitting a mode that is halfway between speaking and writing, the email voice is often much more relaxed, less concerned with correct and precise expression. (Instant Messenger communications—IM—are even less formal, and text messaging on your cell phone is about as informal as you can imagine. Can you see why this would be so?)[1]

In each of these letters, you write to a different *audience* and assume a different *voice*. Writing to your grandparents to thank them, you write very differently—choosing different words, writing in a different tone—than you do writing a love letter. Writing a thank-you note is often a little difficult; how do you say "thank you" without sounding cheesy and insincere? The first few times you write them, it may feel odd. Writing a love letter may have been the easiest to write—you simply write out your thoughts and feelings. Or maybe it is the most difficult; how do you put all of those feelings into words, especially when writing them down exposes you and leaves you so vulnerable? Business letters have still different voices, usually more formal and much less personal. If they are just conveying information, they can sometimes be pretty easy to write. But if you are not sure of your audience—if you don't know personally the person to whom you are sending the memo—they, too, can be awkward to write.

Before the age of telecommunications, though—before telephones, before even the telegraph—letters were the only way to communicate with someone not in your immediate presence. If people generally wrote better in the past (and it is not necessarily provable that they did), it is probably in part because they had much more practice with it. An invitation to dinner to the person across town, a message to one's son at college, whatever—all had to travel by letter. Letter writing was a real art, and people learned it as an art, from books that taught how to do it. This may seem silly today, but for hundreds of years there were books about how to write letters for all occasions: sympathy letters, love letters, letters requesting help from a patron, letters consoling someone after a loved one's death, and so forth. (Some such books are still published every few years.) But on the whole, people learned this art from reading lots of letters and writing the same kinds of letters that were written to them. That is, they learned this art by imitation.

In this chapter, we are going to take you back to one of the great eras of letter writing, the Middle Ages. During this long and fascinating period in history, after the Roman Empire had crumbled and men and women were rebuilding the institutions that are the foundations of Western civilization today, letter writing was crucial. In the collapse after Rome, literacy dwindled, and for a great period of time, only a small portion of the population could read and write. With the general collapse of infrastructure, trade, and exchange across distances that had characterized the Roman empire, communication over distance became difficult. Letter writing was the only way for any administrator—the pope in Rome, kings of France or England or Germany, a bishop or abbot—to communicate effectively across distances which took a great deal of time to travel. Thus letter-writing was a crucial political act; it was tied up with diplomacy, power, rights, freedoms, and, in this crucial time, church-state relations. That is, letter writing was the primary voice of *negotiation*—that complex verbal art where two sides get together to work out differences, share gains, parcel out prizes, and maintain peace. And as with political and diplomatic negotiation today, every word was telling, the phrasing of each sentence important, as these differences were worked out, with the power shared or simply seized.

And if you have worked with us through this book, you are ready for this kind of writing. You are ready to use language that carefully, that self-consciously, in order to move someone in careful negotiation.

Task 7.1

Write a letter to someone where you protest some action he has taken, explaining that what he has done is unjust and unfair. Think of times in school, at work, with businesses, with government employees, and others when you didn't believe you were treated properly. You might think you received a grade you did not deserve, or a boss did not give you the raise you felt you were owed, or some decision went against you, or someone was doing something he should not have done. If you cannot think of such a situation, invent one for yourself. Write it in your normal speaking voice, but show that you are unhappy and tell what you want done about it.

When you are done, bring the letter to class. Read over the letter. Share it with two classmates. What subjects did you choose? What were people ticked off about? Did anyone invent an interesting situation? Together with your partners, try to analyze your voice and your rhetorical strategy. How did you set up the letter? What did you do first, second, and third? Did you try to build up to your complaint, or did you start off with it? What sort of language did you use to convey your anger? Reflect on the process of writing the letter: did you find it difficult or easy? Do you find it easy to express anger and dissatisfaction, or is that not a part of your personality, your writing voice? Next, write for a page or so about this writing experience.

Task 7.2

Read, slowly and carefully, the exchange of letters below between Pope Gregory VII and Henry IV, the German king, in the years 1075 and 1076. It will help to read them out loud, and

I recommend this strongly. There are likely to be words that you have not encountered; look up the meanings of any words you don't know. Take notes on the readings.

First, summarize in your own words what Gregory and Henry are saying;

Second, note any fascinating ways these two say those things—such as interesting turns of phrase or different word choices;

Third, try to describe Gregory's and Henry's voices, using the skills you have learned throughout this book.

Some background before you read:

The conflict here is over "lay investiture," that is, whether the king (a layman) can "invest" bishops with the symbols of their office and thus effectively control who is to be bishop. The modern practice, wherein the pope names each bishop, is far from the medieval practice, which was much more local in nature. At the time, tradition held that other bishops, typically the archbishop of the province, and two other bishops of that province, were to invest the bishop with the symbols of his *spiritual* office (a ring and a crozier) and that the king would invest the bishop-elect with the symbols of his temporal rule. Because bishops often owned huge tracts of land, they could be very powerful politically and economically in a kingdom; as a result, the king thought he should have a say in naming these powerful members of his kingdom. However, the pope affirmed that bishops should be men of God, above mere politics, and for Gregory to reform the church, making it less worldly and more holy, he would have to blunt the king's attempt to gain control over the naming of bishops. (A different—and incorrect—view would say that Gregory wanted to get his fingers into the emperor's politics and wanted to take away some of Henry's power.)

That sets up the exchange of letters. Gregory, whose name before becoming a pope was Hildebrand, is complaining that

Henry is naming bishops himself in the cities of Fermo and Spoleto rather than allowing a free election by the clergy and people of those dioceses. It's not an idle question: if a king couldn't control who was bishop, he might not be able to control his kingdom. The underlying question, of course, is power: Gregory thinks, however, that Henry is stealing power that rightfully belongs to the people, while Henry thinks that the pope is sticking his nose in what should be only the king's business.

Gregory, bishop, servant of God's servants, to King Henry, greeting and the apostolic benediction—but with the understanding that he obeys the Apostolic See as becomes a Christian King. . . .

We marvel exceedingly that you have sent us so many devoted letters and displayed such humility by the spoken words of your legates, calling yourself a son of our Holy Mother Church and subject to us in the faith, singular in affection, a leader in devotion, commending yourself with every expression of gentleness and reverence, and yet in action showing yourself most bitterly hostile to the canons and apostolic decrees in those duties especially required by loyalty to the Church. Not to mention other cases: the way you have observed your promises in the Milan affair, made through your mother and through bishops, our colleagues, whom we sent to you, and what your intentions were in making them is evident to all. And now, heaping wounds upon wounds, you have handed over the sees of Fermo and Spoleto—if indeed a church may be given over by any human power—to persons entirely unknown to us, whereas it is not lawful to consecrate anyone except after probation and with due knowledge.

It would have been becoming to you, since you confess yourself to be a son of the Church, to give more respectful attention to the master of the Church, that is, to Peter, prince of the Apostles. To him, if you are of the Lord's flock, you have been committed for your pasture, since Christ said to him: "Peter, feed my sheep" (John 21:17) and again: "To thee are given the keys of Heaven, and whatsoever thou shalt bind on earth shall be bound in Heaven and whatsoever thou shalt loose on earth shall be loosed in Heaven" (Matthew 16:19). Now, while we, unworthy sinner that we are, stand in his place of power, still whatever you send to us, whether in writing or by word of mouth, he himself receives, and while we read what is written or hear the voice of those who speak, he discerns with subtle insight from what spirit the message comes. Wherefore Your Highness should beware lest any defect of will toward the Apostolic See be found in your words or in your messages and should pay due reverence, not to us but to Almighty God, in all matters touching the welfare of the Christian faith and the status of the Church. And this we say although our Lord deigned to declare: "He who heareth you heareth me; and he who despiseth you despiseth me" (Luke 10:16)....

This edict [against lay investiture], which some who place the honor of men above that of God call an intolerable burden, we, using the right word, call rather a truth and a light necessary for salvation, and we have given judgment that it is to be heartily accepted and obeyed, not only by you and your subjects but by all princes and peoples who confess and worship Christ—though it is our especial wish and would be especially fitting for you, that you should excel others in devotion to Christ as you are their superior in fame, in station and in valor.

Nevertheless, in order that these demands may not seem to you too burdensome or unfair we have sent you word by your own liegemen not to be troubled by this reform of an evil practice but to send us prudent and pious legates from your own people. If these can show in any reasonable way how we can moderate the decision of the holy fathers [at the council] saving the honor of the eternal king and without peril to our own soul, we will condescend to hear their counsel. It would in fact have been the fair thing for you, even if you had not been so graciously admonished, to make reasonable inquiry of us in what respect we had offended you or assailed your honor, before you proceeded to violate the apostolic decrees. But how little you care for our warnings or for doing right was shown by your later actions.

However, since the long-enduring patience of God summons you to improvement, we hope that with increase of understanding your heart and mind may be turned to obey the commands of God. We warn you with a father's love that you accept the role of Christ, that you consider the peril of preferring your own honor to him, that you do not hamper by your actions the freedom of that Church which he deigned to bind to himself as a bride by a divine union, but, that she may increase as greatly as possible, you will begin to lend to Almighty God and to St. Peter, by whom also your own glory may merit increase, the aid of your valor by faithful devotion.[2]

Letter of Henry to Gregory, 1076

Henry, King not by usurpation, but by the pious ordination of God, to Hildebrand, now not pope, but false monk:

You have deserved such a salutation as this because of the confusion you have wrought; for you left untouched no order of the Church which you could make a sharer of confusion instead of honor, of malediction instead of benediction.

For to discuss a few outstanding points among many: Not only have you dared to touch the rectors of the holy Church—the archbishops, the bishops, and the priests, anointed of the Lord as they are—but you have trodden them under foot like slaves who know not what their lord may do. In crushing them you have gained for yourself acclaim from the mouth of the rabble. You have judged that all these know nothing, while you alone know everything. In any case, you have sedulously used this knowledge not for edification, but for destruction, so greatly that we may believe Saint Gregory, whose name you have arrogated to yourself, rightly made this prophesy of you when he said: "From the abundance of his subjects, the mind of the prelate is often exalted, and he thinks that he has more knowledge than anyone else, since he sees that he has more power than anyone else."

And we, indeed, bore with all these abuses, since we were eager to preserve the honor of the Apostolic See. But you construed our humility as fear, and so you were emboldened to rise up even against the royal power itself, granted to us by God. You dared to threaten to take the kingship away from us—as though we had received the kingship from you, as though kingship and empire were in your hand and not in the hand of God.

Our Lord, Jesus Christ, has called us to kingship, but has not called you to the priesthood. For you have risen by these steps: namely, by cunning, which the monastic profession abhors, to money; by money to favor; by favor to the sword. By the sword you have come to the throne of peace, and from the throne of peace you have destroyed the peace. You have armed subjects against their prelates; you who have not been called by God have taught that our bishops who have been called by God are to be spurned; you have usurped for laymen the bishops' ministry over priests, with the result that these laymen depose and condemn the very men whom the laymen themselves received as teachers from the hand of God, through the imposition of the hands of bishops.

You have also touched me, one who, though unworthy, has been anointed to kingship among the anointed. This wrong you have done to me, although as the tradition of the holy Fathers has taught, I am to be judged by God alone and am not to be deposed for any crime unless—may it never happen—I should deviate from the Faith. For the prudence of the holy bishops entrusted the judgment and the deposition even of Julian the Apostate not to themselves, but to God alone. The true pope Saint Peter also exclaims, "Fear God, honor the king" (1 Peter 2:17).

Wherefore, when Saint Peter gave no quarter to an angel from heaven if the angel should preach heterodoxy, he did not except you who are now teaching heterodoxy throughout the earth. For he says, "If anyone, either I or an angel from heaven, preach any other gospel unto you than that which we have preached unto you, let him be accursed!" (Galatians 1:18). Descend, therefore, condemned by this anathema and by the common judgment of all our bishops and of ourself. Relinquish the Apostolic See which you have arrogated. Let another mount the throne of Saint Peter, another who will not cloak violence with religion but who will teach the pure doctrine of Saint Peter.

I, Henry, King by the grace of God, together with all our bishops, say to you: Descend! Descend![3]

Deposition of Henry by Gregory, February 1076

O blessed Peter, prince of the Apostles, mercifully incline thine ear, we pray, and hear me, thy servant, whom thou hast cherished from infancy and hast delivered until now from the hand of the wicked who have hated and still hate me for my loyalty to thee. Thou art my witness, as are also my Lady, the Mother of God, and the blessed Paul, thy brother among all the saints, that thy Holy Roman Church forced me against my will to be its ruler. I had no thought of ascending thy throne as a robber, nay, rather would I have chosen to end my life as a pilgrim than to seize upon thy place for earthly glory and by devices of this world. Therefore, by thy favor, not by any works of mine, I believe that it is and has been thy will, that the Christian people especially committed to thee should render obedience to me thy especially constituted representative. To me is given by thy grace the power of binding and loosing in Heaven and upon earth.

Wherefore, relying upon this commission, and for the honor and defense of thy Church, in the name of the Almighty God, Father, Son and Holy Spirit, through thy power and authority, I deprive King Henry, son of the emperor Henry, who has rebelled against thy Church with unheard-of audacity, of the government over the whole kingdom of Germany and Italy, and I release all Christian men and women from the allegiance which they have sworn or may swear to him, and I forbid anyone to serve him as king. For it is fitting that he who seeks to diminish the glory of thy Church should lose the glory which he seems to have.

And, since he has refused to obey as a Christian should or to return to the God whom he has abandoned by taking part with excommunicated persons, has spurned my warnings which I gave him for his soul's welfare, as thou knowest, and has separated himself from thy Church and tried to rend it asunder, I bind him in the bonds of anathema in thy stead and I bind him thus as commissioned by thee, that the nations may know and be convinced that thou art Peter and that upon thy rock the son of the living God has built his church and that the gates of hell shall not prevail against it.[4]

Task 7.3

Now, take your letter from Task 7.1 and rewrite it, imitating the style and structure of these medieval letters. Then write a response to your letter, again imitating the medieval voice, style, and structure. Try to imitate the style of the medieval letters, from the salutation, to some of the unusual phrasing, to the biblical and religious references. Look at individual sentences and try to imitate their structure and vocabulary. But underneath it all, try to capture the anger and resentment these two powerful, forceful, passionate men had for each other. Have fun, be witty if you like, and as always, take some chances.

To do this exercise, you'll have to go back and re-read the medieval letters very carefully as you write. You'll have to look at the large and small ways that this "voice" is created.

> Look at the macrostructure of medieval letter style; that is, notice the large blocks of structure that set up this voice. I have already hinted at one of them—the odd way of writing the salutation of these letters. Look further: what do these letters tend to do first, second, and third? Look at paragraphs—they are often keys to the large blocks

of thought in writing. What happens in the first, second, third, fourth paragraphs and so on?

Look at the microstructure of medieval letter style. What little turns of phrase make this voice sound as it does? What sort of diction (that is, word choice or vocabulary) makes this sound so different? Are the sentences long and ornate, or are they short and concise? Are they full of similes and images and metaphors, or are they straightforward and flat? Does the writing refer to or allude to other writings (say, the Bible)? What other details make up the sound of this voice? Try to do what they do.

When you are done writing, bring your exchange of letters to class. Share them with two classmates. Read each other's imitations. Did someone write to her boss at McDonald's and try to do it in medieval style? Did someone write home complaining about lack of money and try to make it sound like Pope Gregory VII? Now, compare your letters to the original medieval letters. What different features did your classmates notice and imitate in the medieval letters? What can you learn from their letters that you will want to include in your letters? Notice how the style forced you to contain your anger in a very formal voice—a voice that says, "Yes, I know you are an important, powerful person, and I respect you for that, but you are still doing something terribly wrong, and I'm not going to ignore that." Make some notes for when you revise your letter.

Great Ideas: The Separation of Church and State

The *real* underlying question in this debate is one that has bedeviled Western societies since *at least* the Middle Ages and is still a question today. Does the king, emperor, or other leader get his power from the pope, directly from God, or from the people? Should the pope be subject to the king's political power? In other words, does the king owe the pope anything, is he equal to the pope, or is the pope beneath the emperor (in some senses and not in others)? How should religious authorities be related to secular authorities?

As the noted medieval historian Brian Tierney observes, both Gregory and Henry, but especially Gregory, were working with the idea that government is a unitary enterprise that covers both the spiritual and the secular realms. As he writes, "There is a flaw in this line of argument that was evidently never apparent to Gregory himself. The assertion that ministers of religion have a higher responsibility than secular rulers does not necessarily imply that ecclesiastical officials can depose temporal ones. It is possible to maintain simply that the two structures of offices are separate from one another" (Tierney 56). Neither could really conceive of the idea of separation of Church and State—they were working with an idea that our spiritual values were very much allied with our political life, and therefore spiritual leaders should have a great input into secular leadership. This question, as you can see, was vexed in the Middle Ages; it became still more troubled after the Protestant Reformation, when there was no longer a unified Catholic Church representing the religious leadership. Competing versions of Christianity claimed different viewpoints on the direction a nation should take, and various nations fought bitter religious wars over this issue. In the United States, those who wrote and promoted the Bill of Rights had been influenced by the history of these religious wars, and this was one reason they supported the First Amendment division between secular leadership and religious leadership. You might think that solved the problem, right? Think again: some of the most crucial and heated arguments in American politics today are between "Christian fundamentalists" and "secular humanists" (and many others between and opposed to each) about such questions as abortion, public funding for parochial schools, and nativity scenes in public squares. And there are still countries that have a very close connection between their religious and political leadership—Saudi Arabia, for instance. Clearly Gregory and Henry were debating a fundamental, "Great Ideas" question that has not been conclusively answered in world culture.

Task 7.4

Now revise your medieval letters, trying to get them even closer to the medieval model, trying to make your own voice sound more "medieval." You will probably have to read the letters at least one more time as you write, poring over them carefully for features to imitate. Again, have fun. Bring them to class to show to classmates.

Task 7.5

Write in your journal about this experience. How was writing the medieval letters different from writing the letter in your "own" voice? How did changing the voice and style change what you said and how you said it? What else did you learn from this exercise?

Why We're Doing This

We often write to people in order to get them to do something. We write to complain, to request a refund, to gain admission to college. But as you surely know, the imperative is not often a good mode to use in these situations; you cannot simply order someone to act in the way you wish. These—and many more situations that you encounter in business, in academia, in life— require you to use language carefully, skillfully, *rhetorically*. All will involve negotiation, that art of getting opposing sides to come to some sort of agreement. To be successful with words in these situations, you will have to be supple in your voice, building the macrostructure and microstructure carefully and self-consciously. I end with this selection of letters because I see it as taxing your newfound skills to their limits. By writing in the complex, rhetorically sophisticated style of the medieval diplomatic letter, you stretch your own vision of what it means to use words carefully on an audience. And you encounter another voice—another model to which to apprentice yourself.

Extra Exercises for Those Who Want to Do More

Find collections of letters—by writers, politicians, philosophers, and more—and spend some time reading them. What do you find in these personal letters? How does the letter form enable a certain kind of writing and restrict others? Two of my favorites are the letters of Flannery O'Connor, the great Southern fiction writer, and Evelyn Waugh, the often acerbic English novelist.

Look at letter writing from different periods. How does the form change? Try imitating letter writing from other periods, getting at the conventions of the writing and inhabiting different voices.

Examine business correspondence, academic memos, professional emails. How does each shape its discourse differently? Try imitating each type. Notice the moments of tension and strife and how the writers handle them rhetorically.

How You Can Build Shape Out of "A Mess"

As you noticed through your work in part 1, making a beginning is crucial, so that you have some writing to work with. Getting ideas for your writing is not a matter of divine inspiration, but a matter of generating thoughts and getting them moving around on a page. Through free-writing, through description, through definition, you began to learn how to get ideas, how to reflect on them, and how to begin to give shape to those thoughts.

But sometimes you are still at this stage with confusing beginnings. Thoughts are there, but they have not found their order, their shape, just yet. What do you do? For many of us, apprentices and masters alike, this is a difficult stage of writing.

You should notice that, if you have completed all of the tasks in the chapters up to this point, you *have* learned these skills; you have learned how to build from a "mess" into something coherent and organized. Let's look back over what you have done and discover what you have learned by apprenticing and imitating your way through this book.

You already know some forms. If your job is to write a set of rules, or a thesis-driven argument, you no longer have to agonize about the shape and structure; you know several options. If nothing else, you should have noticed by now that *most writing tasks have conventional and prescribed forms built into the task.* Memos tend to look pretty much the same; companies' annual reports have a standard form. The boss who asks you to write a report does not expect you to reinvent the wheel; he has a form in mind, and it is up to you to find previous examples of this and learn what its prescribed forms are. So if you find you have a task whose shape you do not know—say a report, or a movie review, or something else—you know what to do: find other versions of this kind of writing and analyze its macrostructures and microstructures.

When I am talking about making a shape out of a mess, I am largely talking about **macrostructure**, the larger blocks of thought which help lead your readers through your ideas. And here in this section you have not only learned different **genres** (types of writing, the largest macrostructures out there), but you have learned the parts of these parts.

But you have also come to realize, I hope, that you can begin by generating material that already has a shape. Even your invention work need not start with simply open, unstructured free-writing, but even in that free-writing you can begin shaping the ideas towards writing a report, a movie review, instructions, or a formal argument. That is, you have a set of samples to imitate as you work in the future, like the pattern book a carpenter consults so that he does not have to figure out how to build a staircase or a table all over again every time.

Writing is not just "forming"—shaping ideas as you write according to their inner logic—but "con-forming," fulfilling the logic of the prescribed form, the standard genre, as you write.

But you might also look at what lies behind these genres and macrostructures, for I have not taught you every genre out there, and as you write in the future, you will need to learn more genres and how they work if you are going to be a flexible, competent writer. For instance, you by now have surely noticed that these different genres fulfill different **purposes**, do so for different **audiences**, and therefore take different shapes or organizing features. You write instructions to help people accomplish a task; this is different from writing to persuade someone to agree with or do something. And therefore the audiences for whom you write in each situation are different, as are the ways you organize these two kinds of writing.

The genres I had you attempt in this section are ones that prize standard organization. A description can in some ways begin anywhere and end anywhere, and an essay is almost by definition a meandering tracing out of your thoughts. But if you are proving a point logically, it obviously becomes important what you put first, second, and third. And if you are persuading someone of a complex point, you will have to be very careful indeed how you lay out your points, how you appeal to emotion, and more.

So as you come upon a new writing situation, and you have assembled a "mess" that needs organization, you can know that you are not without skills. You will know that one of your first steps is to analyze the purpose of your writing. What do you hope to achieve by the end of this piece? Why? How can this help you make some order out of the mess? Further, you know you will have to analyze the needs of your audience. What does your audience know and not know? In what ways are they likely to have trouble—following your directions, following your proof, with the idea you are putting forward for their agreement? What will make them confused, angry, displeased? As you answer these questions, you will begin to see what you must do first, second, and last.

But the other thing you will begin to recognize—and this is where I believe this book sets itself apart from others—is that you do not need to invent all of this for yourself, *ex nihilo*, every time you write. Because you have apprenticed yourself to these other writers, to these genres, you will have a stock of organizing practices that will help you get started. And you will have already practiced them, because you imitated them in this section of the book. You've got a tangled mess, for example, and don't know where to start next, but you realize you are writing a logical argument? Good—you come back to this chapter and remind yourself how those arguments work, and you go about putting together a good argument.

And this holds true not just for macrostructure, but for **microstructure** as well. Maybe you will imitate not just the organization of an annual report, but also the specific language choices that make a report sound professional, that make *you* sound like a professional when people read your reports.

So this is the point of how this book works—you learn by imitating, building up a stock of examples in your head, so that the next time you are confronted with a similar situation you can build an organized structure out of the unfocused mess. You do not have to "reinvent the wheel" every time; you rely on the tradition of accomplished masters who have gone before you. And if the situation is different, if you find yourself writing in a genre we have not covered here, you know what to do—find good examples of that kind of writing, analyze it for its macrostructure and microstructure, and imitate it until you learn how it works.

Task 8.1

Reflect on what you have learned from the chapters in Section Two, paying particular attention to structure and organization. What do you notice about your ability to build from "a mess" into something coherent? Is it becoming easier for you? Are there still tasks that are difficult? (If so, don't worry; as we said, this is one of the most difficult tasks for all writers, beginner to expert.) Consider, that is, where you were before working on this section and where you are now. And what do you still have to learn?

Task 8.2

Consider a time in the past when you had a "mess" of good ideas but no sense of where to take them. It could have been a paper for some other class, a letter to write to a friend, or some other writing situation. If you were confronted with the same situation today, what would you now know to do that you did not know then? What would you do first, second, and third to give the writing a "shape"?

Task 8.3

Think about how you might write in a genre we haven't covered here. For instance, how would you write a movie review? There you probably begin with a "mess"—your initial, unfocused reactions and evaluations of a movie—but may not have an idea of how to organize it into something with a shape. How could the material you've practiced in Section Two help you? For instance, must you define anything? Are you trying to persuade your audience? Of what? What kind of an audience? Write for a bit on this. Then find several examples of the genre—again, just for example, of movie reviews—and see if you can learn from professionals how to give your movie reactions a shape.

Setting Up Shop for Yourself: Leaving the Workshop and Becoming a Master

Art begins in imitation and ends in innovation.

–Mason Cooley

For most of human history, and in most cultures, people learned skills and professions not through formal schooling but through an apprenticeship. A person did not go to school to become a blacksmith, or a carpenter, or a tanner or musician or painter; he found a master, apprenticed himself to him, and learned the craft of the trade through long years of working at the master's side, starting with basic tasks and working up to be able to perform the skills the master had. You, too, have now apprenticed yourself to some of the great masters of writing: ancient, medieval, modern, and contemporary. You have learned basic skills like description and definition, refined those skills, and learned to master some of the complex moves of contemporary writing. Now it is time to leave behind your masters (for now), hang up your own sign, and become a writer yourself.

It can be a little stressful. It probably was for the medieval blacksmith first hanging up a sign with an anvil outside the shop in his small village, stepping out on his own, wondering if his work would be good enough to attract customers, if he could feed his family on his own rather than with what he received from his master. But he knew he had prepared well. So have you. If you have worked through this book, you do not know everything about writing well, but you are ready.

For an apprentice to become a master, he had to create a masterpiece—remember, not the "greatest work of his career," as we use that term today, but the *first* piece of work good enough for him to be considered a *master* in his own right. It was scrutinized by other masters in his guild, and when it passed their examination, he was welcomed into the guild and fully licensed to open his own shop. So remember—the goal of this book is not for you merely to produce clever imitations and/or parodies of other great writers. That has been merely the means, the practice, to give you the skills to be able to write well in all writing situations that you may find in the future.

That is where you are now. You have the ability to sound like some of the greats; by now, you should be able to take just about any kind of writing, break it down, and imitate it. In so doing, you have come to realize the deep learning that goes on when you perform an imitation. That is an astonishing accomplishment, and you should be justly proud of your newfound abilities. They will stand you in good stead as you move out into the world of business, academia, or elsewhere.

But the real accomplishment would be to take the next step. I heard a blues harmonica player once say that he had spent his youth studying and learning to play like all of the great harmonica players of the past. But then, he realized, "Nobody was going to pay to hear me play like all those other guys. I had to play like *me*." The process of discovering what he sounded like—his own harmonica *voice*, if you will—was, he said, the most important step, but he could not have done it without learning from all of the greats of the past.

So it is time for you to produce your own masterpiece, to show that you have arrived and are ready to join the ranks of the accomplished writers. You will not do this by thinking about it; you will have to *write*. So as we come to the close of this book, here are some suggestions for taking that next step.

Task 9.1

Write for about four or five pages in your own voice. Choose any topic, and just sound like yourself. You can be cheerful, you can be angry, you can curse, you can write whatever you like— but make your writing sound like your natural voice, like *you*. Someone reading this should be able to hear *you*—the lively, interesting, fascinating person you are. Are you a sarcastic type? Are you a serious, organized person? Do you love puns? Do you tend to be irritable and curmudgeonly? Are you a dreamer? The observant reader should be able to sense those things in your writing.

You may have found this at the outset more difficult than you thought it would be. After imitating all these other voices, it can sometimes be hard to find or remember your own voice. Or it might be easy; after reading and imitating all these others, you might have come to realize that your voice is close to a master's or that you sound nothing like any of them. Often it takes a few pages to find your natural voice—that is why I suggested you write for four to five pages. If you are still struggling to find your voice, or even if you are not, try looking through your history of writing to see how your voice has evolved.

Task 9.2

Find some other samples of your writing. You can find any- thing—a lab report for another class, a paper written earlier in college (or even high school), a short assignment, a full-fledged research paper, a piece written for the newspaper, a letter to friends or relatives. It is best to find several examples, written over a span of time, written for different purposes and audiences. Look them over carefully, then write about the following questions:

> *What does your writing voice sound like? How does it work? To what or whom would you compare it?*

> *How many different voices do you have?*

> *How has your writing voice changed over the years?*

> *Use the concepts of macrostructure and microstructure to help you answer the above questions.*

> *Are there places in the writing that do not sound like you? What are they? Why do they not sound like you? Try to describe or explain these parts. Were you straining to say something that you were not comfortable with? Were you hedging on the truth to please a certain audience? Was there some other reason you shifted into another voice?*

As you begin to discover your own voice, you are beginning to discover what sort of shop you will set up, what masters you will choose for continuing influence, what sort of writing life you will have. As you begin to discover your voice(s), it is time to begin work on your masterpiece. The idea here is to produce a major piece of writing, one that you feel would be acceptable not just in a class but out in the real world: the world of business, or academia, acceptable to a boss or editor or director. Beginning to take your writing this seriously is the first step. It should be a kind of writing that *you* choose—not because it has been assigned to you—and by which you announce to the world that you are no longer an apprentice, but a master.

Task 9.3

Think about, and free-write about, the kind of writing you would like to do for this major project. You might wish to work on a project that is part of your major in college—perhaps producing a marketing plan for a product, a scientific report, a legal brief, or a piece of literary criticism. On the other hand, you may wish to explore a kind of writing you have always wanted to do but have never had the time to set forth. Perhaps you are a business major who has always wanted to write poetry, or a biochemistry major who has always wanted to try writing movie reviews, or an English major who is tired of literary criticism and wants to write fiction yourself. You might find in the chapters above short examples of things you would like to do yourself.

Or consider your passions, the things that really drive you in life. It could be a political passion, or an issue of social importance, or a hobby. What drives you? Where do you find yourself spending your free time? If you had no other commitments, what would you do with your time? How could you write about it? Free write about these things and see where they might lead you to a writing project.

One of the marvelous things about this exercise is that it builds on the work we have been doing yet opens up an entire world to you, and perhaps might point you in the direction of future careers and lives. As the theologian and novelist Frederick Buechner has said, "Your vocation is where your deepest happiness meets the world's greatest needs." That's a wonderful statement, for it affirms that the things that make us happy—avant-garde music, soccer, Renaissance art, linguistic theory, marketing plans, messenger RNA—are keys to what we might do in life, if we can use them to help the world be a better place. (Watching hours of ESPN on the couch might make some of us happy temporarily, but it is probably not going to make us deeply happy, and it is not exactly going to meet the world's greatest needs; we have to remember both poles of Buechner's statement.) I once had a student who was somewhat embarrassed and ashamed because, unlike some of her equally successful peers, she had no desire to go to graduate school; she wanted to teach English and coach women's basketball in a small town in Missouri. I quoted her Buechner's statement, and asked: "Would teaching and coaching make you happy? Would it serve one of the world's great needs? Then do it. We need as many good high school English teachers—no, more—than we need Ph.D.'s in English." I could see a wave of relief come over her, as if she needn't press so hard to be someone else. Your writing should be this way, too; as you move out into the world, there will be some writing you do because you must (memos, thank-you notes), but you should strive to make your writing come out of your passions and be directed at the world's needs. At least for this project, you should try to engage the kind of writing you would like to do, something that makes you happy in this deep sense. If you find that kind of writing, you will put in the long hours to make it professional, to polish it.

But what does any of this have to do with the imitation exercises we have been exploring throughout this book? Now it is time to put this into practice.

Task 9.4

Find several samples of the kind of writing you would like to try. You might have to consult with professors in these majors, or professionals in the field, to get some good examples. Now, using the same skills we have practiced throughout this book, analyze how the writing works. Consider macrostructure and microstructure. Consider rhetorical organization; look at ethos, pathos, and logos, for instance; watch how terms are defined and how the writing describes the reality of its subject. The more samples you can find and read carefully, the more your knowledge will grow.

Now, write for several pages—as long as it takes—a detailed analysis of how this writing works. Do all the examples work in the same way? Is there a common macrostructure, but many different microstructural differences?

❧

We are almost there. Now we are at the stage where the harmonica player had studied all of the great masters of the blues harmonica. (Of course this study took him several years, so do not think that this will be an easy step, particularly if you are studying a complex form of writing.) The next step will create your masterpiece and show that you are ready to become a serious writer.

Task 9.5

Produce your own writing, inventing, drafting, and revising until you believe it to be your "masterpiece," the work that will show that you belong in this world of writers. Make it look professional, from the paper you choose to use to the formatting to the care with which you proofread it.

You may wish to hew closely to the kind of writing you are studying, particularly if the audience expects it—in scientific reports, for instance, or marketing studies. On the other hand, you may wish to modify or reject the conventions of this kind of writing and honor your own individual voice, but you do so with the knowledge of how this writing ordinarily works and what risks you take in deviating from these norms.

Take your writing and show it to the "masters" of this particular profession. What do they think? Is it professional in quality, in approach, in vision? If not, what does it lack? What have you still to learn about work and writing in this field?

If the professionals think it is a "masterpiece," congratulations. You are ready to join the working world of real writers. (If not, you should not feel crushed; the standard length of an apprenticeship in older cultures was seven years, so you may still be on the road.) Remember, of course, that even accomplished writers never stop studying masters, never stop learning from the greats, whether they are novelists, poets, dancers, or jazz musicians. They go back to that well for refreshment, for new ways of seeing and understanding, for new macrostructures and microstructures to imitate and make their own.

❧

It is time to leave the apprentice's workshop. You have the tools, the crafts, the skills. You will spend a lifetime honing them, learning new moves, exploring new areas of knowledge, finding new voices to express your thoughts as you change as a human being. But you have the foundation, the framework, and now can set up your own shop, take in apprentices, and return the gift by teaching them your knowledge. Welcome to the Writer's Guild.

Appendix

Free-Writing: A Primer

Part One: Free-Writing—A Catechism

What is free-writing?

It's an invention technique—a way to get your thoughts going and get some things down on the page so you have material to think about, stuff to push around, ideas to combine and refute and puzzle over and develop.

Why free-write?

Freddy Krueger in all of those terrible *Nightmare on Elm Street* movies. A great white shark with his mouth open, swimming towards you. What's more terrifying than either of these? How about a blank white page (or these days, a blank computer screen) staring back at you? Many of us freeze up just from the thought of having to come up with something to write about, and we're not alone: the fear produced by "writer's block" (or even the fear of someday having it) has driven many a writer to drink, drugs, or worse. You need some method to just get yourself going. Free-writing gives you that—a way to get something, *anything* down on the page or typed onto the screen, so you get a start.

Most writer's block is caused by some form of perfectionism—the thought that you can't write *that*; you can't possibly say *that*. It's terrible! It makes no sense! Under this illusion, the writer believes he can't say anything until it's good enough, or just right. So he rejects ideas before he even gives them a chance, aborting them in the womb before they have had any time to develop.

The way around this? The honored and beloved poet William Stafford said it best: "Lower your standards, and start again."

So, how do I free-write?

Get out a piece of paper or turn on your computer, and start writing. Set a timer—for five minutes, ten minutes at most—and just write for that time. Keep going for the whole time. That's it.

You mean write about anything?

At first, yes—about anything. Later you can give yourself a topic: my thoughts about that Medieval Literature class today, what I think of the latest congressional activities, Plato's forms, the topic for an upcoming paper. But first just get used to writing this way about anything. Spew. Complain. Whine. Exult. It doesn't matter. Many writers I know start their day by giving themselves a couple of pages just to whine and rant and complain. Once they do that, they're warmed up, gotten the crankiness out of the way, and can start their writing day.

Are there any rules?

Right now, none. Just write.

Really?

Well, no, there are no *rules*. But there are some suggestions that have helped writers in the past learn to free-write productively, to wit:

Keep the pen moving. Write the entire time. Don't stop, look up, look around, read what you've written. Just write. If you're typing on the computer, you must do the same—keep those fingers clicking on the keys.

If you can't think of what to write, write, "I can't think of what to write." If, at the end of writing that, you still can't think of what to write, write "I still can't think of what to write." Pretty soon, trust me, your mind will present something to you, even if it is just "I don't get the point of free-writing." Good! Now you can write about that.

Don't worry about spelling or punctuation or any of those concerns with correctness right now. Later you can fix that—right now we just want to generate stuff.

Follow your nose. If you find yourself writing about something off the topic, don't worry about it—follow that instinct. You might surprise yourself with what you write. If this starts to play itself out, gently come back to the topic.

Go for the jugular. No one has to see this, or will, if you don't want him to. So write what you really think, the radical, fundamental truth as you see it.

Why do I just keep writing? Shouldn't I think about it, engage critically with it?

There will be time for that later. In the first stage of free-writing, you're just looking for your freshest thoughts, that part of your mind that generates ideas and questions and problems and answers. You're trying to defeat The Editor. You know him, don't you? The Editor is that little voice in your head that looks at your writing as you are starting, and says, "Did you spell that correctly?" and "Is that really what you mean?" and "Are you sure?" and "Mrs. Jones from English class wouldn't think that was good," or worse, "What would your mother think if she knew you wrote that?" The Editor is interested in correctness and precision, and he has a good place in writing, but this is not his place—you can let him do his work later. If you let him rule you now, he'll stop you dead in your tracks.

So how to defeat The Editor? Write rapidly and keep going. The Editor will always want you to stop and fix something. "Wait—that was supposed to be a semicolon!" "Oh, really?" you say, "Sorry—I'm on to the next thought." "But—but—you misspelled. . . ." "That's fine," you say, "I don't care about that right now; I care about what I'm trying to get to here." See, The Editor is interested in going backwards, and right now at least you just want to go forward. "Who cares?—I'm working on a cool idea here," you say. Eventually The Editor just gets frustrated and says, "Well, *fine*—if you're not going to listen to me, I'm going away." And you say politely, "Thank you; that's what I wanted."

For some people with particularly strong Editors, it may take a few times to defeat him or annoy him enough that he goes away, sulking on the sidelines. Persevere. Write rapidly. I promise, he'll go away pretty soon.

But isn't correctness important? You're an English professor, and you're telling me not to worry about punctuation and spelling?

Yes, that is what I'm telling you. Because when it comes to generating ideas, those things are not important. Later, after you have drafted your ideas and are starting to work them up into a polished piece of writing, when you have your imitation pretty far into the process, you can give The Editor free reign—that is when he is helpful, and when he is at his best. And you'll need a fully developed, obnoxious Editor at that point to pick apart your prose. Good writers know this, and their Editors know it, so they wait patiently for their turns. But again, now is not his turn.

How much should I do?

Try free-writing for ten minutes at first. Later you can build up to fifteen or twenty. Don't think of it as wasted time, even if nothing practical comes from it at first. If nothing else, you are loosening up those writing muscles, like an athlete warming up before the track meet.

> *Isn't this the opposite of imitating your way to good writing? Aren't I just spewing my own thoughts, and not disciplining them by imitating the great masters?*

At this point, yes, that is what you are doing. But to imitate the greats, you will need to have some ideas, some subjects, some *stuff*, to work on. In each chapter you work through in this book, you will need to come up with your own subject matter to work into an imitation—a set of rules, a Thomistic question to "prove," a "defendant" for your Ciceronian imitation. This is a good method to use for coming up with those topics. Once you have some topics, set aside this method and start in on your imitations.

Part Two: Double-Column Free-Writing

This is a more developed type of free-writing that gets you beyond those first thoughts and starts you into reflecting upon and developing those first thoughts that free-writing generates. It has been used for years by many of the best writing instructors across the nation, and I have used it in my classes for many years, to great success.

Take out a piece of paper and draw a line down the middle of the page. For ten minutes, free-write on the left hand side of the page. Follow everything you learned about free-writing above.

Now, set another timer, this time for, say, fifteen minutes. Go back and start re-reading what you wrote in the left-hand column. As a thought, a question, a problem occurs to you, free-write it in the right-hand column. Maybe it will be a single question; maybe it will be a comment or two; maybe you will get going and fill up the entire right-hand column with your questions and reflections. Then, whenever you have exhausted that thought, question, or comment, go back and pick up reading the left-hand column again. When another thought occurs to you, start writing in the right-hand column again. Go through the entire left-hand column in this way, adding comments, questions, extensions, and reflections in the right-hand column.

Now you have not just those first, fresh thoughts off the top of your brain, but a second layer of thinking, more reflective, perhaps more critical, more questioning. Now you have not just ideas, but some development of those ideas.

You can even add a third column and free-write again, reflecting on your reflections. My friend Keith Rhodes (the bass player from the "To the Student" section at the beginning of this book) says that when he's written about five columns, he knows exactly what he wants to say, and even has pretty good ideas about how he will say it, how the argument will be structured, and so forth. He maintains that since he started this method he actually writes more, and more rapidly—multiple-column free-writing is actually more efficient than his old, laborious way of developing ideas, because he quickly gets to his points by reflecting upon reflections.

Try it. I have found many students over the years who have found this a helpful tool. One was skeptical about the technique when I taught it to her class a few semesters ago; it seemed gimmicky, she thought. But she tried it and then decided it worked. By the end of the semester she told me, "Now I start all my papers this way."

Works Cited

Achebe, Chinua, *Things Fall Apart* (New York: Anchor Books, 1959).

Alan of Lille, *Anticlaudianus, or The Good and Perfect Man*, trans. James J. Sheridan (Toronto: Pontifical Institute of Medieval Studies, 1973).

Aristotle, "Poetics," in *The Basic Works of Aristotle*, ed. Richard McKeon (New York: Random House, 1941).

Augustine, *On Christian Doctrine*, trans. D. W. Robertson Jr. (Indianapolis: Bobbs-Merrill Co., Inc., 1958).

Barr, Stephen, "Faith and Quantum Theory," *First Things*, March 2007.

Budziszewski, J., *Written on the Heart: The Case for Natural Law*, (Madison, WI: InterVarsity Press, 1997).

Buechner, Frederick, *Wishful Thinking: A Theological ABC* (New York: Harper and Row, 1973).

Buhle, Mary Jo, and Paul Buhle, eds., *The Concise History of Woman Suffrage: Selections from History of Woman Suffrage*, ed. Elizabeth Cady Stanton, Susan B. Anthony, and Matilda Joslyn Gage (Champaign, IL: University of Illinois Press, 2005).

The Catholic Study Bible, gen. ed. Donald Senior (Oxford: Oxford University Press, 1990).

Chesterton, G. K., *Heretics* (London: John Lane Company, 1905).

Chesterton, G. K., *The Man Who Was Thursday: A Nightmare* (London: Penguin Books, 1968).

Cicero, *Selected Political Speeches*, trans. Michael Grant (London: Penguin Books, 1969).

Corbett, Edward P.J., and Robert Connors, *Classical Rhetoric for the Modern Student*, 4th ed. (New York: Oxford University Press, 1998).

Crider, Scott F., *The Office of Assertion: An Art of Rhetoric for the Academic Essay* (Wilmington, Del.: ISI Books, 2005).

Dickens, Charles, *Great Expectations*, ed. Angus Calder (London: Penguin Books, 1965).

Dickens, Charles, *A Tale of Two Cities*, ed. Richard Maxwell (London: Penguin Classics, 2003).

Eliot, T. S., "Tradition and the Individual Talent," in *Selected Prose of T. S. Eliot*, ed. Frank Kermode (New York: Farrar, Straus and Giroux, 1975), 37–44.

Geoffrey of Vinsauf, *Poetria Nova of Geoffrey of Vinsauf*, trans. Margaret F. Nims (Toronto: Pontifical Institute of Medieval Studies, 1967).

Grant, Michael, ed. and trans., *Cicero: Selected Political Speeches* (Baltimore: Penguin Books, 1969).

Haswell, Richard H., *Gaining Ground in College Writing: Tales of Development and Interpretation* (Dallas, TX: Southern Methodist University Press, 1991).

Hemingway, Ernest, "A Day's Wait," in *The Short Stories of Ernest Hemingway* (New York: Scribner Paperback Fiction edition, Simon & Schuster, 1995), 436–39.

The Holy Bible, Containing the Old and New Testaments (Chicago: Gideons International, 1962).

Horner, Winifred Bryan, *Rhetoric in the Classical Tradition* (New York: St. Martin's Press, 1988).

Joyce, James, *A Portrait of the Artist As a Young Man* (New York: Viking Press, 1964).

The Magic Schoolbus Collection, Warner Home Video, 2003.

Milton, John, *Paradise Lost*, 2nd edition, ed. Scott Elledge (New York: W. W. Norton & Co., 1993).

Oxford American Dictionary, ed. Eugene Erlich et al. (New York: Avon Books, 1980).

Shakespeare, William, *The Merchant of Venice*, in *The Riverside Shakespeare*, ed. G. Blakemore Evans (Boston: Houghton Mifflin Co., 1974), 250–85.

Shakespeare, William, *The Tempest,* in *The Riverside Shakespeare,* ed. G. Blakemore Evans (Boston: Houghton Mifflin Co., 1974), 1606–38.

Stowe, Harriet Beecher, *Uncle Tom's Cabin, Or Life Among the Lowly* (New York: The Modern Library, 1938).

Thomas Aquinas, *Summa Theologica,* 5 vols., translated by Fathers of the Dominican Province (Westminster, Md.: Christian Classics, 1948).

Tierney, Brian, ed., *The Crisis of Church and State, 1050–1300* (Toronto: University of Toronto Press, 1988).

Virgil, *The Aeneid,* trans. Robert Fitzgerald (New York: Vintage Books, 1990).

Walcott, Derek, *Omeros* (New York: Farrar, Straus and Giroux, 1990).

Ward, Geoffrey C., Ric Burns, and Ken Burns, *The Civil War: An Illustrated History* (New York: Knopf, 1990).

Weaver, Richard M., *Ideas Have Consequences,* reprint version (Chicago: University of Chicago Press, 1984).

Wright, Richard, *Native Son* (New York: Harper and Row, 1940).

Notes for Teacher Use

Notes for chapter 1

1. As we begin this first chapter using modeling or imitation, I want to work from the students' strengths, or at least from their own experience, so I begin with this assignment akin to free-writing. (For more on free-writing—how and why to do it—look at the appendix.) Encourage the students to relax and not worry too much about excellence at this point; remind them that this preliminary assignment is only to help them begin the work of this chapter. You may introduce invention strategies at this point so that students can explore subjects for their descriptive writing; since they are likely to have a ready supply of subjects, a simple brainstorming exercise ("List people you know well/unusual people you know/people who generate a strong emotional response in you") will be sufficient. What you will find in this first assignment are the students' difficulties and lack of abilities in description. They will often begin this assignment with some confidence only to discover how difficult a task description can be. Thus I strongly *dis*courage grading this first assignment.

2 This is probably enough information for the students, but instructors may want a bit more information about Geoffrey, so I want to provide it for you here. The work was written sometime early in the thirteenth century. Geoffrey was probably an Englishman; he studied at the University of Paris and taught at Hampton in England. He is clearly trying to write a guide in the tradition of the pseudo-Ciceronian *Rhetorica ad Herennium*,

for poetry to him is one of the branches of rhetoric. As Margaret Nims notes in her introduction to the translation, Geoffrey believes that poetry comes from "*ars*—a thorough knowledge of the rules; *imitatio*—the study and imitation of great writers; and *usus*—diligent practice" (9). I couldn't agree more, though I get to those three goals somewhat differently from the way Geoffrey does.

3   This may be to some students, and some instructors, a troubling, even sexist, description of a woman. On the other hand, anyone who knows medieval aesthetics will see here a high medieval Platonism at work, where Geoffrey is exploring not a specific woman but a kind of abstracted form of Woman. There is a great deal here to analyze in terms of politics and ideology if you wish to do so, and students may very well be interested in such a discussion at this point. It is up to you as an instructor to decide how much of a place such a discussion will take in your classroom. As I am at this early point focused more on technical skills of syntax and diction, I tend to look at these things briefly and then move on, though I do open up at this point the intersection and inseparability of form and content.

4. I strongly recommend that you do not work through these selections with the students before they have attempted their first draft imitation. Let them struggle and flounder with them. Again, this is learning by doing. Let them try to imitate Geoffrey on their own before walking through the selection. Students need to take a stab at this themselves. Though they often look at this passage and say (even aloud to the teacher), "What the heck is this?" often they surprise themselves with how much they can do. I strongly recommend that you don't take that away from them. Later there will be time for working through the passage in class—a crucial step that I will cover next. Students come back to class after a few days away working on this exercise with varied reactions. Some are baffled and just happy to have gotten something down; others are excited and joyous, having never been given the chance to do something like this in school before, and a little intrigued by what they have done. Most of them are somewhere in between; they may have had fun trying a turn of phrase or two but frustrated by a great deal of the exercise. It helps if the teacher reassures them (a) that this was a difficult exercise; (b) that the idea was to try, to take chances, to explore; (c) that there's no need for the imitation to be perfect at this point; and thus that (d) any reasonable attempt to make an imitation of the passage is a good start. Only after they have struggled with and attempted to imitate the passage should you analyze it with them in class. It is helpful to begin the class after

their first attempts by asking, "What features did you notice and attempt to imitate?" By letting the students discover some of the features for themselves, they begin to build their own skills in reading and analyzing complex prose.

5   As you begin to analyze the passage with the students—indeed, with all of the models in the book—I have found it useful to speak about **macrostructure** (the larger sections and structures of a work, often the overall design and features a paragraph or larger) and **microstructure** (features at the level of the sentence or smaller: syntax, diction, metaphor, metonymy, etc.). This has worked well in enabling students to see how a selection "works," how the author has built up the passage. You might discuss how macrostructure limits the microstructural choices, or the opposite: how, in any given macrostructure (the business memo, the persona letter), there might be many "voices" created out of choices at the level of microstructure. Another question might be whether or not one should use technical rhetorical terms: should you teach students what *occupatio* is, or *gradatio*, or distinguish between metaphor and metonymy? I leave that for you to answer based on your own abilities and pedagogy. (One good on-line source for learning rhetorical terms is "The Forest of Rhetoric," presently at http://humanities.byu.edu/rhetoric/silva. htm.) Sometimes students enjoy learning the technical terms and distinctions between them; other students find these baffling and a barrier to understanding. On the whole, I find students like knowing the technical terms and getting to know 2,500 years of rhetorical tradition; doing so does not "murder to dissect," but gives students the concepts and language to perform more careful analysis. I will offer the following advice: do what works to improve their writing, and do not quiz them on the terms—if they are interested enough, they will make this vocabulary their own, *on* their own.

So let's look at this passage from Geoffrey and explore what you might discuss with the class.

೩೪   **Macrostructure** is pretty simple and straightforward here, and a good way to discover the reading-skill level of your students. Most of them should have seen that Geoffrey suggests that description proceed from head to toe. If they do not see that on their own, you will need to help them read more slowly and with a greater eye to structure.

The features of **microstructure** here are interesting. Students surely should notice that the sentences often start in the subjunctive, with "Let the . . ."; the class might profitably discuss how Geoffrey asks Nature to fashion this description, creating, in effect, an ideal human being based on a kind of Platonic pattern-mold of "woman." Students should also notice and imitate the constant use of comparative techniques—metaphor and metonymy—in the description: "smoother than polished marble let Nature fashion her chin . . ." Each body part is not merely itself, but emblematized by some feature of the natural world. Syntax: students should attempt to imitate Geoffrey's balanced phrasings, his constant use of apposition ("her eyes, those watch-fires of her brow"), and his tendency to complex sentences: a single main clause with dependent clauses attached. Above all, Geoffrey achieves the effects he seeks through repetition of phrasing and diction. Often students have been told that *variety* is the key to good writing: here you might begin having them see that repetition (and then, repetition with variation) is often the mark of a distinct and lively voice, especially within the Western classical rhetorical tradition.

Students will also want to notice the constant way Geoffrey invokes the Golden Mean—but also the deviations from it, usually in the direction of smallness: Geoffrey's ideal woman is small, slender, with "tiny feet." (Some classes enjoy discussing at this point historical and cultural variations in the notions of feminine beauty: one might compare not just Rubens and the images in *Mademoiselle*, but also Marilyn Monroe's rather *zaftig* features as compared to the more recent "waif" or "heroin chic" look in models.)

A feature that in some ways skirts the boundary between macrostructure and microstructure is the **modesty topos**. Many students miss it, but good readers will notice from the beginning that Geoffrey's description skips from the waist to the legs—and yet in appealing to the reader's imagination ironically emphasizes the genitalia even more. Students might want to reflect on the cultural differences that allow Geoffrey to describe breasts and yet employ the modesty topos here.

6. I strongly encourage you to give the students time to participate in a workshop in class; it is helpful to them to see others' attempts, successes, and failures, and to discover features that partners may have noticed and imitated that they did not. Then I recommend that you provide the students at least one chance to **revise** their first imitation efforts. Students are likely to be somewhat chagrined at the number of features they missed and eager to imitate more closely Geoffrey's techniques. As they revise, their confidence soars; what seemed extremely difficult to them when they first read the passage now seems achievable. You may offer that opportunity now, or later, if you are considering using

a portfolio-influenced grading system. But I recommend encouraging them to revise now, so that they see that imitation builds from first perceptions to more complex ones, and so that their confidence thereby increases.

7. The first Dickens passage is a masterpiece of economy in description. Before students go home to read and attempt the passage, you may wish to read aloud in class a bit more of the novel merely to give them a context for this passage. But have the students focus carefully on the paragraph beginning "A fearful man . . ." and encourage them, now in their second attempt at imitation, to analyze it closely before beginning to imitate.

   After they have attempted their imitations, discuss some of the wonderful features of the passage.

  स Students are often shocked to find that all three sentences are fragments; this is a good place to explore how great writers break the "rules" creatively. The first sentence moves from a general description that seems to be a "first impression" ("A fearful man") to the general nature of his dress ("all in coarse grey") to the crucial detail that establishes Magwitch's status as an escaped convict ("with a great iron on his leg"). Students will be challenged to imitate these features in their own description—the first two are relatively easy, but the task of thinking about the crucial detail that summarizes the person's character (what Eliot might call the objective correlative) is worth some time.

  स The second sentence continues the pattern of the first: a man with . . . and with . . . and with . . . Pip first looks up (to the head, with no hat), and then down, to the shoes, and up again to the head; here Dickens seems to mimic Pip looking Magwitch up and down, as if to attempt to come to grips with him. Students can and do imitate this feature well.

  स The third sentence in some ways follows the rhythmic pattern of the first two, but this time it substitutes relative clauses: A man who had been . . . and . . . and . . . and . . . and . . . then shifts: who [verbed], and [verbed], and [verbed], and [verbed], and whose . . . Students should be directed to note the difference from the earlier two sentences (in that these do not directly describe physical attributes) and to imitate this sentence structure carefully and precisely. Here Pip notices the actions that must have produced the features he is seeing: "lamed by stones, and cut by flints" and then proceeds to the actions Magwitch is currently displaying: "who limped, and shivered, and glared and growled." Help students to see this difference between the metonymic description of the first half of the sentence and the focus on current action in the latter half.

❧ Dickens's diction is, as often is the case, quite simple and straightforward. Notice how few words are Latinate in origin, how many of these are one-syllable words. For students who might think "good writing" means elaborate or abstruse writing, Dickens is a bracing tonic.

It is worth asking students what picture the reader assembles from these details and to discuss how this works, the reader assembling the general picture from the individual concrete details like a portrait from mosaic tiles, or, as discussed in the Great Ideas section, like a scene from the brush strokes of an Impressionist painter.

8. The second Dickens passage—the description of Mrs. Joe—has astonishing complexities, many of which students will likely never master. But even in their trying they will learn a great deal, and accomplished students can approximate some of the wonderful features here. Let's look together at some of these features:

❧ Some students may not see that the **macrostructure** of the description reveals something interesting: Dickens describes not just Mrs. Joe, but embeds in the middle a marvelous description of Joe Gargery himself. The description moves from the adroit use of the pun, "brought up by hand" (meaning, literally, bottle-feeding rather than breast-feeding), applying it first to Pip and then to Joe, and then to the ironic of the apron. Both involve taking a figurative use of language and treating it literally: "by hand" moves from its figurative sense of nursing to the literal application of Mrs. Joe's hand to Pip and Joe, and the apron complaint, which Mrs. Joe means figuratively, Pip then takes literally: why doesn't she just take it off, if it annoys her so much to wear it? If students can do these three—begin with a pun, embed a description of a second character, and then end with an ironic use of a third objective correlative—then they will have learned a great deal from this passage.

❧ The **microstructure** features become almost too numerous to mention, but a few should be noted here:

o Students might be instructed to notice how the balanced sentence structure works as a counterpoint to the relaxed, almost musing way the description appears to proceed. Students may think that these details are merely tumbling out of Pip's brain (and thus Dickens's pen) in a random order, but they need to be shown how carefully controlled this effect is. If students struggle, they can begin merely by plugging in: "My _____, Mr/Mrs. ____ ____, was more than _____, and had established a great reputation with _____ because he/she had _____ _____." Soon they will loosen up and begin imitating, not just mimicking.

o The description of Joe is in many ways old-fashioned: a straightforward description of his physical features followed by a list of adjectives that culminates in the paradoxical comparison to Hercules. Linking them here is the fascinating description of his eyes, which seems to lead from one sort of description to the next.

o Mrs. Joe washing herself with a nutmeg grater may be obvious to some students and obscure to others, who may not have ever seen whole nutmeg or know why it might need to be grated. Again, it might be worthwhile to point out to students that this type of description is a species of *metonymy*—here, a substitution of the cause for the effect. Students often at first think they will not be able to invent an appropriate metonymy of their own, then surprise you with splendid or sharp or caustic or hilarious metonymies, once they understand how one works.

9. I offer these sections on "Great Ideas" so that students can see some of the wider context for what they are attempting. In my own classes, I have found that students particularly enjoy these excursions; they take the class out of the realm of pure technique and help them see these techniques in historical and cultural perspective. They find themselves linked better to a world of "real writers," writing, and ideas. My own discussions here in the text are by necessity brief; I encourage you to develop them as you wish and according to your own interests. Here, for instance, an instructor with an interest in art might bring in slides of Impressionist paintings; another might copy a selection from Conrad for the class; another might add in a discussion or debate on the questions I raise. Still another might want to invite an art professor to class to explore how he or she explores imitation, modeling, and creativity in studio classes. Do people still try to paint like Monet? Is there any value in at least learning how to do so?

10. I encourage you not to skip this reflection assignment in any of these modeling/imitation chapters. This way of learning to write will be quite foreign to many of the students, and these texts will have been different, challenging them in quite new ways. Students will want to vent, to explore, to think about what they have been doing; they need some time to reflect upon these unusual assignments. As an instructor, these can be important times for you to gauge whether the notion of *imitatio* is making sense to your students, or whether the entire process is merely puzzling them.

11. I have said it pretty clearly here, but I encourage you to emphasize this point in class: good writing comes from good reading, and a great deal of it. I can only provide a start here with a few choice selections, but all writers spend their lives reading, absorbing, modeling, and imitating. Still, if they have understood the process, students can choose any piece of writing that fascinates them, and, through imitating, analyzing, and imitating some more, apprentice themselves to many more masters.

Notes for chapter 2

1. I do strongly suggest that you take these chapters in sequence, but I know enough about writing teachers, including myself, to realize that often instructors choose from among the chapters available in a text and/or create their own sequences. Still, I give these introductory words to show the students that these skills being learned are not random, but are part of a carefully built sequence.

2. What I am looking for here is some situation where the student can describe the setting, actions, and speech of several people over some interval. I begin with minutes precisely because they are dry records of actions, and I want the students to see how much is left out of minutes and how much else there is to be described. In my first times teaching this chapter, however, I realized the gulf between teacher culture and student culture: instructors and professors are constantly attending meetings and thus reading minutes, but many of my students had a difficult time finding the minutes to any meetings they had attended, or else had attended no meetings for which minutes were taken. So do expect students to come to you with this problem, and allow a certain lattitude in this first assignment. As long as they have some description of an event that can later be transformed, it will be a start. One possibility is that you could have the student write about an event that would in no

way be called a "meeting"—for instance, a Thanksgiving dinner with her family—and for this assignment render it in the form of minutes: "At 4:30 P.M. the Family Patriarch called the dinner to order. The Family Matriarch then led the assembly in prayers of thanksgiving. Committee reports were heard from the Family Members At College committee. . . ." I have not provided a sample of minutes here, expecting that virtually every student will have seen what minutes look like, but if you encounter some who have not, I recommend that you provide the students with xeroxes of minutes from some recent meeting you have attended so they can learn the conventions.

3. Hemingway works well here for a number of reasons: he is somewhat familiar to students; his stories pose no immediate problems of Latinate syntax or difficult diction, yet have subtleties that are worth noting; his style is distinctive and can be imitated well; and he shapes his world in unique ways. Because of this, I have encountered little trouble teaching this story or this section of the book. I chose this particular story because it seems to offer in a brief compass and yet an artistic whole many of Hemingway's chief gestures and ideas.

4. As always, I encourage you to let the students imitate on their own first before you work through the story as a class. They will learn a great deal, and you will learn a great deal about their reading and writing abilities, if they attempt to imitate the story first on their own.

5. I repeat these instructions for each chapter in case students are encountering this material for the first time, and to remind those who are not what questions they might wish to ask.

6. Students who have had some experience reading fiction critically may not have much trouble seeing the macrostructure at work here, but others might have more difficulty.

  ᴈ◍   I suggest you begin by looking at the story through the classic Aristotelian structure of exposition, complication, climax, and denouement, so that students can see how Hemingway has built a full narrative movement in this quite short story.

  ᴈ◍   Another pair of terms that has been helpful in teaching this story is the one the New Critics often used, the difference between *scene* and *panorama*. For Allen Tate and Caroline Gordon, *panorama* was the equivalent of a long shot in film, events described from a dis-

189

tance and covering a certain span of time, while *scene* was a shot from up close, focusing on events slowly and carefully and slowing down time considerably from the way panorama covers time. Students may need to be shown that the story opens in scene, moves out to panorama for the doctor's visit, moves back to scene, moves back out to panorama for the time the narrator goes hunting, then returns to scene for the rest of the story. It is the alternation of these techniques that keeps the rhythm of the story working well.

ॐ Students may or may not have been introduced to the concept of point of view, so it would be worth showing them how this artistic decision is a crucial part of any story's macrostructure. I will not bore or insult you by offering here an elementary lecture on point of view in narrative, but students need the vocabulary of "first person," "third-person limited omniscient," etc., to help them discover the importance of point of view. A brief five-minute lecture or a one-page handout can give the students what they need quite easily.

7. Hemingway's style, frequently parodied, comes largely from the features I have been calling microstructure, and they are worth some real attention as you conduct class discussion. I do not pretend to be exhaustive, but among the things you might discuss with your students are the following:

ॐ Hemingway's simple syntax. Many of the sentences here are simple, a few are compound sentences, and even fewer are compound-complex sentences. You can analyze a few of them to show how rarely Hemingway employs more than one dependent clause in a given sentence.

ॐ Hemingway's simple diction. This is a marvelous time, if you have not yet introduced it, to show the students the difference between Anglo-Saxon and Latinate diction (which I admit is a rough, crude distinction, but a workable and useful one). Given the choice, Hemingway almost always prefers the Anglo-Saxon term to its Latinate synonym.

ॐ Hemingway's brief, alternating snippets of dialogue, each speaker rarely speaking more than a simple sentence at a time. Students may not see how revolutionary this was until they look back to Victorian novels and short stories in which speakers tend to hold forth at greater length.

ə♥ Hemingway's lack of attribution (in most cases). In my experience, students come back from their first attempts at imitating this story with attributions ("she said," "he noted") scattered all over the page, and only after it is pointed out to them do they realize that in the story Hemingway omits many of these. Students are often surprised to see that they understood perfectly well who was speaking, despite the lack of attribution, because of the convention of beginning a new paragraph each time a new speaker talks.

ə♥ Hemingway's reticence about naming or discussing emotions, which forms so much of that male, even macho sense in Hemingway's fictional world. The father here does not emote over his child, and although we get a sense of the boy's fear, even it comes out indirectly throughout much of the story. Students who can begin to approach imitating this feature of Hemingway's style are doing very well indeed.

8. I have left this interlude as a possible in-class exercise, but I strongly urge you to have your students attempt it as they work on imitating Hemingway's style, which so relentlessly favors "showing" over "telling." I usually perform this exercise first with one student in front of the entire class. This allows the others to see how it works before they practice it. It might also be a good idea to have students do practice after class, turning in to you some "showing" they produce after watching another person for ten minutes in, say, the cafeteria.

ə♥ Another possible exercise in showing: tell the students that you are going to walk out the door of the classroom, then walk back in. They are to describe—to "show"—everything they see you do. As you walk back in, perform obvious actions (slam the door, drop some papers, trip over a chair leg) as well as subtle ones (utter a small sigh, fiddle with a piece of paper, sit oddly in the chair). At some point, stop and tell the students: "Now, go. Describe what you just saw. Don't *tell* what emotion I was just displaying, but show what you saw and heard so your reader will experience what you just experienced."

9. The selection from the opening of *A Portrait of the Artist As A Young Man* often provokes strong reactions in my students and may in yours as well; Joyce's style still has that ability to shock and delight and disturb even almost a century later. Yet it is also not as difficult as it may at first

appear, and most students understand the passage pretty quickly. A few things you may wish to point out to them include:

- **Macrostructure** may not be obvious to the students at all if they are looking for traditional prose divisions, but there are still features that are worth considering, including time and point of view. You will want students to notice, for instance, where Stephen moves from describing the external world to his own thoughts, whether memories or musings. In their own imitations, you may have to nudge the students toward including more of this internal dialogue, and to show how it happens associatively—some external object or act prompting some memory or idea, or conversely, some memory bringing the speaker's attention back to the external world. In fact, if the students have a hard time seeing this, five minutes working on the old "word association" game can get them to see how Joyce's poetics here is tied to a Freudian notion of the subconscious and even unconscious.

- How Joyce handles time is of course a crucial part of this structure: we begin with the memory of being told a story and move through successive memories as Stephen works gradually outward into the consciousness of others and their lives. Then we move ahead to the scene at the playground—the "present," perhaps?—and yet continue to shift into more recent memories (the conversation with Nasty Roche, the memory of Cantwell's retort, his mother and father saying goodbye to him on his first day at the school). We end with Stephen looking ahead to the end of the holidays.

- Most students want to include snatches of songs in their imitations and to imitate the young child's mispronunciations.

- Of course, there is a great deal of dialogue in the passage as well, and students should not merely submit narration. The rhythm of narration and dialogue is as important here as it was in Hemingway, and you should encourage students to imitate this, too.

- **Microstructure** fascinates the students. They enjoy imitating the opening sentence (justly one of the most famous in literature), but they may not at first realize that, with only a few exceptions, Joyce builds his prose here on short, clipped sentences.

- In the Hemingway assignment students may not have noticed the absence of speaker attribution, but here, since Joyce uses dashes to indicate a quotation rather than quotation marks, the students may pick up on the stylistic oddity more quickly.

This is not the place to enter into a full-scale discussion of literary theory, but then again, perhaps students will want to know a bit about signs and signifiers, Derrida and his critics, and a whole Western tradition that has debated these questions for some time. In my own classes, I refrain from going too far into this discussion—not from a lack of interest in it, but because I wish to keep the focus on improving the students' writing. Thus, I ask the students about their own perspectives on the relationship between reality and language, or by asking them whether they find Hemingway or Joyce more attractive, closer to their own personal voice. Without going into much literary theory, one could push the discussion a bit further simply by asking the students about their reactions to metaphor and opening up Lakoff's and Johnson's *Metaphors We Live By* to show the students how much of language is metaphorical. One of the things I like about teaching in this way is that such questions arise not out of the abstract, but out of the actual practices the students must confront.

10. I probably should not say this—it will not sell me any more books—but the assignments in this chapter in particular could be applied to any narrative writer, and you could choose your own pieces for the students to imitate. If you do, I urge you to start with strongly contrasting voices, as I have here, and work toward more subtle differences, as I suggest in suggestion number three below.

Notes for chapter 3

1. If you wish, you might here have a short traditional workshop on definition, introducing how definitions work by naming the genera (the general category to which something belongs) and then by distinguishing it from all things in that generic category: "A dog is a quadruped that . . ." This, of course, is the *stipulative definition;* you might also introduce definition by analogy and by example. But I encourage you not to overdo it; much better to allow these questions to emerge from the imitation exercises themselves, and even to allow the students to stumble in their first attempt at definition.

2. For those who prefer a more modern translation, here is the *The Catholic Study Bible* version:

Excellence of the Gift of love. [1]Now I will show you the way which surpasses all the others. If I speak with human tongues and angelic as well, but do not have love, I am a noisy gong, a clanging cymbal. [2]If I have the gift of prophecy and, with full knowledge, comprehend all mysteries, if I have faith great enough to move mountains, but have not love, I am nothing. [3]If I give everything I have to feed the poor and hand over my body to be burned, but have not love, I gain nothing.

[4]Love is patient; love is kind. Love is not jealous, it does not put on airs, it is not snobbish. [5]Love is never rude, it is not self-seeking, it is not prone to anger; neither does it brood over injuries. [6]Love does not rejoice in what is wrong but rejoices with the truth. [7]There is no limit to love's forbearance, to its trust, its hope, its power to endure.

[8]Love never fails. Prophecies will cease, tongues will be silent, knowledge will pass away. [9]Our knowledge is imperfect and our prophesying is imperfect. [10]When the perfect comes, the imperfect will pass away. [11]When I was a child I used to talk like a child, think like a child, reason like a child. When I became a man I put childish ways aside. [12]Now we see indistinctly, as in a mirror; then we shall see face to face. My knowledge is imperfect now; then I shall know even as I am known. [13]There are in the end these things that last: faith, hope, and love, and the greatest of these is love.

Again, I encourage you to have the students work through their own attempts at imitation before you help them analyze the passage. Let them struggle through a first attempt and see what they discover; let them work with others to see what others discovered. Then bring the class together and solicit their ideas—what they noticed, what they tried to imitate. As you begin to work through the text with them, you might notice some of the following (I make no claim that this is an exhaustive list of features, only that these might be some of the more helpful features for the students to try to imitate):

Macrostructure. Students who vaguely remember the passage might be surprised at the length of the example, wondering why I did not begin with verse 4, where the definition proper begins. But encourage them to see that the definition really does begin with verses 1–3, which offer three negative definitions of *caritas* before the text launches into the definition proper in verses 4–8. Even in these verses Paul advances a largely negative definition of *caritas*: he explains what it is by telling us what it is not as much as he tells us what it is. You should also ask the students to consider what verses 9 (really, 8) through 13 do to advance the definition of *caritas*. My answer: they are an attempt to define the eternality of *caritas* by showing what are all the things that will fail or fade away at the end of time.

You should also engage your students in the rhetorical situation in which Paul finds himself. Why, given what we know about the Corinthian community, does he use a negative definition here? Why, that is, must he show them what charity is *not* before showing them what it *is*? Students who understand this will then have a much greater appreciation of the rhetorical craft of a good definition and how it can and should be employed in different ways for different rhetorical purposes and different audiences.

ह **Microstructure.** One of the chief reasons I have chosen this particular passage is its wealth of sentence types, patterning, structure, and rhetorical figures. The KJV committee knew its classical rhetorical figures and deployed them well here, and a student who imitates these sentences will have a much better command of English sentence structure than before, even if he cannot name the devices and even if he cannot parse the grammar of what he has done.

ह Start with the first three verses, and get the students to see the similar, yet slightly varied, sentence structure: "Though I x (and x.1 and x.2), and have not y, I am/have z, (or z.1)." Then add in the smaller features: the synecdoche of "tongues of men and angels," for instance. If students can craft sentences like these—again, I insist, *even if they cannot name the parts of what they are doing*—they will have improved their writing by significant degrees and will in the future notice and hear these sentences in their heads as they write in other contexts.

ह You might discuss changing attitudes towards punctuation when you come to the colon in verse two: according to modern handbooks, this is an improper use of the colon.

ह As you move through verses 4–7, have the students imitate the way the passage increases its rhythm by shortening the clauses. In fact, after verse 4, the subject (charity) is elided. In verse 4, we alternate from two positive definitions ("suffereth long" and "is kind") to three negative definitions ("envieth not," "vaunteth not itself," and "is not puffed up"). Verse five consists entirely of negative definitions, while verse 6 has a negative then a positive definition, leading to the four quick positive definitions in verse 7. The pace of these lines comes from the use of *epistrophe*, the rhetorical figure where one ends a series of clauses (or poetic lines) with the same phrase.

    Conversely, verse 8 employs *anaphora*, the figure of beginning successive clauses with the same phrase; in fact, the verse comes very close to *symploce*, the combination of *epistrophe* and *anaphora*. Verse 9 similarly is virtually *symploce*, with only the verbs varying ("We x in part, we y in part"), which sets up the variation in verse 10, a variation that depends on the balance and opposition thus created. Verse 11 returns to epistrophe in its first half to set up the contrast in the second half.

    One figure students seem to enjoy imitating is the *asyndeton* of verse 13 ("faith, hope, charity"—there is no "and" separating hope and charity), asyndeton meaning "without a connector." This is a wonderful rhythm students can use again and again in their writing once they understand how it shapes a list. And one can discuss again how the "rules" of good writing—"one must always separate the penultimate and final items on a list with a comma and 'and'"—are violated regularly by superb writers, writers who yet depend on those "rules" in order to break them creatively and with great effect. One can also at this time teach *polysyndeton*—the figure of using *too many* connectors. You might ask the students to determine which way might be most effective: the grammatically "correct" way, the text's use of *asyndeton*, or a use of *polysyndeton*: "faith and hope and charity."

As far as rhetorical figures go, then, these are rather simple ones, yet by having the students focus on these microstructures you introduce them to some sophisticated notions about writing, get them thinking in new ways, and create the sound of complex sentence structures in their heads, a sound they will never lose.

3. I encourage you to get the students to generate material at first. Ask them: what did you notice that you wanted to imitate? As they begin to call them out, write these features on the board, then go back and organize the discussion according to microstructure and macrostructure, providing the technical terms if you like.

4. Truth's speech is truly a wonder, an extemporaneous yet carefully crafted response to many of the charges—she must have known them by this time as well as one knows any cliché—leveled against women in the nineteenth century. As you work through the speech with students, they may not see at first that the entire speech rests on a critique of the prevailing definitions of a woman. So the first task will be to break down the macrostructure to see this well.

Truth begins with a twist on the well-known "if there's smoke, there must be fire" cliché—you might wish to help the students see how simply shifting the terms of a cliché can help it regain some freshness. She locates the "smoke" or "racket" as being about "rights," but then asks what the deeper question behind the question of "rights" is. And thus the rest of the speech is about this deeper question: the definition and description of "woman."

She first takes on the definition, "woman is someone who is physically helpless." Students may need to see that she lays out the opposing definition before refuting it with the facts of her own life, then asking her famous question. That is, she shows that she, clearly a woman, is counterfactual to the definition. In so doing, she leads implicitly to a new definition of woman.

Her next point may seem odd at first. Rather than denying the charge that women lack intellect, she rules the issue out of bounds: what does this have to do with a woman's rights? That is, she seems to understand that a frontal assault on this question—especially from a woman with little formal education—would not be effective. So she suggests that the equality of humanity lies deeper than mere intellect, and that fairness lies in recognizing each person's own gifts, however extensive or limited. One wonders how many in the audience, surely accustomed to judging intellect in the terms of formal education, immediately recognized that her rhetorical tactic shows her intellectual agility. The passage works, then, by questioning or at least modifying the long-held Aristotelian definition of man as "a rational animal" and attempts to root it in something deeper.

But it is perhaps Truth's attacks on the supposed biblical reasoning for antifeminism that are the most effective, given the rhetorical situation in which she found herself. By reminding the audience of what they already knew—Joseph's at best marginal role in the parentage of Jesus—she redefines the role of woman in biblical thinking. And by turning Eve's supposed weakness into her strength, she again offers up a definition of woman as strong and forceful.

If students can see how she takes up each point of the previous definition of woman and inverts them, through a macrostructure of questioning and response, they will go a long way to understanding how, like Paul, Sojourner Truth commands rhetorical power through her subtle use of definition.

5. I am compelled to make a point about the use of the "n-word" here. You will notice that the transliterated version, taken from another edition, turns this into "Negroes" below. After long consideration, I decided to use the much more volatile and offensive term here in the interest of historical accuracy. It would appear that Truth indeed said "niggers," as far as history has been able to ascertain, which is what one would expect, knowing what we know about African-Americans' self-descriptions at the time. In preserving this historical accuracy, I make no brief for the use of the term by twenty-first-century people of any race. If you so desire, this can be a fascinating place to have a discussion about how small choices of diction (and indeed other aspects of microstructure) can have wide and important repercussions rhetorically, politically, and personally; one might discuss the controversy over Quentin Tarantino's frequent use of the "n-word" in *Pulp Fiction*, as well as Samuel L. Jackson's defense of Tarantino's diction. In addition, one could have the students read—or one could excerpt for their reading—Randall Kennedy's recent book *Nigger: The Strange Career of a Troublesome Word*.

6. There is a great deal to be said about microstructure here, but much of it the students will ascertain on their own without a great deal of discussion. Yet a teacher might wish to point to how Truth's speech works so well at least in part because of her excellent employment of rhythm—both the rhythms within her sentences ("ploughed, and planted, and gathered into barns," each phrase gathering syllables) and the rhythm between sentences. What she employs, of course, is the African microstructure of call-and-response, in which the speaker's statements call forth spontaneous expressions, verbal and nonverbal, from the audience; the responses urge the speaker on, encourage her, answer and complete the speaker's statements, fill in information, and ultimately, powerfully affirm the speaker. By asking a question—here, "ain't I a woman?"—the speaker calls forth the answer that she desires. Thus Truth leads her audience, through call-and-response, to affirm her definition of "woman."

Students should be encouraged to find these small moments of rhythmical phrasing and to imitate them. A student who can do this will find her sense of sentences growing and will begin to anchor her own writing in such rhythms, whether or not she can apply grammatical and syntactical terms to them—as, surely, Truth could not when she spoke these words.

7. This can be an enormously valuable part of the experience of imitating. As the students ponder their work, they consolidate what they have learned, come to understand why they have performed this odd exercise, and begin applying it to new areas. I encourage a very flexible attitude to evaluating and assessing this material. For the most part I suggest that you just make sure the students are treating the assignment seriously and honestly and avoid assigning page limits or critiquing what is written here. Instead, just respond, if you must, as an interested and helpful coach.

Notes for chapter 4

1. This is perhaps an unpopular view among academics today, but I hold that there is a difference between apparent authority and real authority, between authoritarianism and genuine authority, and the latter resides in those who speak not just with rhetorical power but with a true assessment of the nature of things. If you disagree, you are welcome to discuss this with your students; in fact, this entire chapter, where I deliberately choose for imitation a text that is at the center of the "culture wars" in the United States, can become, if you wish, the occasion for an extended discussion about issues of power, authority, language, and rhetoric. I do not duck the issue in my own classes, but again I tend to let it arise out of the students' own attempts to create for themselves a voice with authority. That is, I put the writing first, and trust that as the students work towards learning the writing skills they will almost inevitably be forced to confront the cultural and philosophical issues inherent in their uses of language.

2. It is important that the students have a good, fairly lengthy set of rules for this exercise, so they can see how it transforms when put into the King James voice. Almost any organization will do—a sports team, a fraternity or sorority, a campus or community club.

3. As I noted above, students may have intimate knowledge of the Ten Commandments, a vague notion of them, or perhaps no experience with them whatsoever. All, however, can find new things by reading the passage closely and carefully. A few things you might call to the students' attention, *after* they have attempted the imitations on their own:

ॐ **Macrostructure**

   o The selection begins not with the first commandment per se, but with Yahweh announcing his identity and his history with

199

his people. Few students, interestingly, note this on their first imitation—that the rules come not from a disembodied voice, but from a particular and personal point of view. And of course this is crucial, for it at once establishes Yahweh's authority and his personal relationship with the "people of the desert."

o After this, the macrostructure is not difficult; it is, after all, a list. But there are some items on the list which get more attention than others, or at least more development, and some which are stated simply and clearly. You might ask the students to think why some commandments (the Sabbath) get a great deal of attention, while others need only a brief, direct reference (stealing). What does this convey to the original audience? To an audience today? If students can imitate the rhythm of this passage, beginning with longer explanations and narrowing to short, pithy commands, and ending with the final sentence that combines related prohibitions, they will be imitating well.

Microstructure

o Students need not be overwhelmed by "thou" and "thee" if the instructor explains to them that these are the Elizabethan personal pronouns. Some may be fascinated to learn that "thou" and "thee" were the more personal forms, equivalent to the Spanish "tu" form, and "you" is the more formal address, equivalent to the Spanish "usted" form. Thus Yahweh is addressing his people, at least in the King James Version, not on a formal basis, but as an intimate. For students used to conjugating verbs in a foreign language, putting a typical chart on the board might help a great deal with first-person, second-person, and third-person singular and plural. In addition, showing students the difference between the subject pronoun ("thou") and the object ("thee"), as well as the possessive pronouns ("thy" and "thine"), will go a long way toward demystifying these archaic forms.

o The voice is achieved here largely by carefully balanced phrases: from the simple, as in "that love me and keep my commandments" (v. 10), to the more elaborate succession of "or" or "nor" phrases, as in verses 8 and 14. If you have not had opportunity to discuss them, this is a fine place for a brief discussion of independent and dependent clauses, coordinating conjunctions, and hypotaxis vs. parataxis, for the distinctions are clear here and powerfully displayed. By imitating, the students will intuit these distinctions, but giving them a name may also be helpful.

o Have the students pay particular attention to diction—not just the archaisms, but the contrast between the simple muscularity of the diction in some places (v. 11) and the somewhat more elaborate diction in others. Students should strive to find ways to translate their own sets of rules, which are likely to have much more pedestrian diction, into the powerful choices made here.

4. The exercise suggested in this brief note—brainstorming the ways students are already authorities—is a useful one to do in class for many reasons. It bolsters students' confidence, especially those first-generation college students or others who struggle to find their voice in a world where they seem to know so little. Furthermore, as I have suggested above, it generates a marvelous stock of topics for future papers. Often, for students struggling to find a major and discover a vocation in life, this list can begin an even deeper process of self-exploration as they discover what they know, what they are good at, and what they enjoy doing. Students often need your encouragement to realize that, not only do they have something to say, but they can indeed say more intelligent things about the topic than you can. Any honest and decently confident composition teacher admits that she learns a great deal every semester about subjects well beyond her own experience; a child of the suburbs myself, I learned during nine years of teaching in small Midwest towns a great deal about hunting laws and policies, the economics and politics of agribusiness, and the difficulties of rural public schooling, to name only a few topics, all from freshman composition papers. Students need to know this, and they need to learn how they can establish and build their own authority in their writing.

Notes for chapter 5

1. This is one place where the question of parody may arise. In the past, I have had students offer topics like "Are chocolate-chip cookies better than oatmeal-raisin cookies?" As I noted in the "To the Teacher" section, parody can be an important pedagogical method if controlled properly, and a playful, intelligent, humorous Scholastic argument may teach as much as a serious one. On the other hand, parody can become an excuse for refusing to take seriously the learning going on in this chapter. I do wish to emphasize the serious nature of the students' quest for truth and knowledge. An overemphasis on parody can turn *imitatio* into a mere sophistic exercise of clever manipulation.

2. Here I have included another reading that is sure to be controversial in the classroom, and I make no apologies for that; in fact, given the events of September 11, 2001, and their aftermath, including the wars in Afghanistan and Iraq, this very argument—on the various interpretations of the term *intifada*, on the proper response of the United States to the attacks, on the Israeli-Palestinian conflict—has been at the center national and international debates. While I could have chosen a *questio* from the *Summa* that is (to modern ears) much more abstruse and abstract—such as whether the universe has always existed—I have decided to include one in which the relevance is immediately obvious and which could provide for vigorous classroom debate, if you so desire. At the very least, students can see in one of its classic and best-argued forms a position that is often alluded to but rarely so carefully stated, and then discover for themselves their own positions on this question. My emphasis again is on the writing, on the students learning careful logical macro- and microstructure, and out of that learning to make careful logical distinctions themselves, so that the product of this chapter is not merely their debating Just War Theory, but their learning to argue logically many other topics as well.

3. If students have been working through the book chapter by chapter, they should not feel quite as daunted by this piece. Yet they will still find it difficult and need some time to revise carefully and fully. After they have attempted an imitation the first time, you will need to work through the question carefully. Here are some—though not all—of the features you may wish to explore with the students.

    ▪   **Macrostructure.** This is a kind of writing that highlights its structure in many ways, and therefore the students should first and foremost work towards grasping how this structure works.

        o First, of course, the Scholastic proof is based on a carefully worded *question*. Have the students notice how Aquinas states the question—not "can a Christian fight in a war?" but "is it always sinful to wage war?" The *always* and *sinful* are the crucial terms for analysis here. Work with the students, showing them how rewording their own questions can produce very different kinds of issues and proofs, and how controlling the question is a powerful rhetorical move. An illustrative example is provided by the abortion issue, where one side asks the question, "Is it ever right for the government to interfere in a woman's choice of what to do with her body?" while the other asks, "Is it ever right for a woman to take the life of a child, even if it happens to be inside her own body?"

o Aquinas's method is interesting and based on university practice: first he handles the objections—that is, the opposing views—then states his "answer" or own position on the question, and then, one by one, gives arguments opposing each of the objections, signaling each of these carefully in his text. If students find this incomprehensible, remind them that Aquinas is to a great extent merely reproducing his class notes—that is, how a disputed question would work in his own classes, where he would allow the "con" side to speak first, then the "pro" side, and then give his *determinatio*. The only difference is that his *determinatio* is given in the middle of the argument. Accustomed to stating their own positions first and then handling objections to their arguments, students at times get this structure reversed. But I believe that learning Aquinas's structure properly is crucial, and this is one of the fundamental reasons I have included Aquinas as a "master" to whom one should "apprentice": he shows that one fundamental, and perhaps temporally prior, step in formulating one's own arguments is to understand the opposing side's arguments as fully and completely as one can.

o The Scholastic argument is almost universally *deductive* in nature, and this one is as well. Aquinas proceeds from a few key terms and understandings—war, sin, the political good—and takes his argument from there. You may wish to explain to your students the difference between inductive and deductive arguments at this point. Or it may be useful to return to definition and see how important a careful definition of terms can be in an argument.

ə▶ **Microstructure.** Students will intuit some of these features themselves, but here are a few things on which you might concentrate:

o Logical connectors, tags, and signals: to produce his arguments, Aquinas must signal the logical relationships quite clearly with tags such as "furthermore," "therefore," "nevertheless," and more. If students can begin to see these not merely as questions of "correct grammar" but important logical signals, they begin to see why mastery of elements like coordinating and subordinating conjunctions is so crucial in their writing.

o Citation of proof texts: as part of the deductive logic of the Scholastic argument, students will see that Aquinas roots the ultimate authority for his argument on the Bible and crucial church fathers, especially Augustine. Building on chapter 4, which considered authority in making rules, students should be encouraged to see how citing authorities adds weight to an argument (as well as the limitations of doing so). They should consider what the proper authorities for their own imitated arguments might be. If you are allowing parody, students can have a delightful time inventing authorities for their positions, but you should ensure that the parody is appropriate and not just absurd. Even a parody of a logical argument should in its own way foreground a logical argument.

o Logic per se. Though I defer to colleagues in philosophy and mathematics who may be much better at teaching this than I am, I must say that in my own experience, teaching students the rules of logic in an abstract way is no more helpful in making them better *writers* than teaching them grammar in an abstract, decontextualized way: much of what is taught is quickly forgotten, gets tangled, and becomes counterproductive. Furthermore, as E. D. Hirsch has noted in *The Schools We Need and Why We Don't Have Them*, there is little empirical evidence that such instruction gets carried over into other disciplines or in fact into real life. Thus I have omitted long discussions of the various modes of syllogism, the square of opposition, or logical fallacies. Furthermore, about the only practical use I see in this teaching in writing classes is to get students to detect fallacies—and perhaps have them learn to use the fallacies craftily on others, or accuse others of using the fallacies. Instead, I maintain that humans are inherently logical (for the most part) and only get into trouble in those rare instances when subtle and fine distinctions must be made. For this assignment, I encourage instructors to resist a lengthy lecture on logic, and use instead an approach of applied common sense, having the students analyze the argument for its first principles and then proceed to see if the argument makes sense. If you wish to introduce the technical terms of Aristotelian (or other systems of) logic, you may do so, but I encourage its immediate application to the writing at hand and the logical connections between clauses, sentences, and paragraphs, so that the focus remains on the writing.

Notes for chapter 6

1. If you have been using the chapters in sequence, you will see that there has been a definite change in the last two chapters. We have been working from directing others and establishing one's authority towards that complex rhetorical task of establishing a thesis and persuading others of it. The scholastic argumentation in chapter 5 should have provided the students with a very strange, hyperdetermined argumentative structure. The very idea of proving a point so carefully is something many students have not heretofore encountered—and proving a point in such a hyperstructured macrostructure is something that few if any will have seen before. Many students report that using the scholastic form forces them to consider counterarguments as they never have before. In this chapter, I move from that foray into argumentation into what should seem a more familiar structure. You might encourage the students to see that Cicero's oration is, in many ways, like the standard academic essay that composition classes (and their high school English classes) have been attempting to teach them to write. Weaker students, I have found, are often weak precisely in that they cannot see that there is a structure to this kind of writing—and while it is not as hyperdetermined as the scholastic proof, it is nevertheless a consistent structure that shapes how the thoughts will be presented. If by the end of this chapter students can indeed see that the seemingly fluid oration of Cicero has a structure— and that this structure has a rhetorical purpose and determines the shape of the thought—they will have come a long way towards becoming accomplished writers.

2. I do find that students' appreciation, interest, and comprehension of Cicero is enhanced by a discussion of Roman civil life and rhetoric's place in it, and I encourage you to spend just a few minutes on this topic. Also, the emotional valences of the word "argue" vary widely among students. This is partly a cultural matter; students from the Northeast, for instance, are often much more comfortable with arguing as a pleasurable activity than students of staid farm stock from, say, Wisconsin, for whom arguing might be seen as rude and impolitic. Furthermore, a certain unthinking relativism needs to be confronted here, as the difference between mere opinions and informed opinions is often not clear to students.

3. When I began teaching this particular imitation, I expected that students would arrive at this reading and find it at long last a familiar kind of writing—an essay with an introduction, body, and conclusion—and

therefore come to the reading with some relief and a higher measure of comprehension. Not so. I was surprised to find that students report that they are as confused, if not more so, by Cicero as by any of the other readings. Part of this could be the length of the reading; I find that some students just give up after a certain length. But more likely it is Cicero's diction and Latinate syntax that lose students; students with little syntactical sophistication will soon find themselves lost in the layered, complex sentences here. Encouraging them to read aloud—and reading aloud yourself to the class with exaggerated expressiveness so that students can catch Cicero's irony, sarcasm, and idealism—will often make those complex clauses fall into place.

4. I do not expect all who teach this chapter to be experts in the field—this time, classicists. I am not one myself. I have chosen this text, in fact, because it has been such a common one in beginning or intermediate Latin classes, and am hoping that at least some might have a familiarity, however fading, with the text. Cicero's career and thought is well documented and studied, though, so for those who need background there are many resources. Teachers at schools that still have one of the diminishing number of classical languages programs might enjoy inviting a classicist for a guest lecture. However, the text is relatively clear once one knows the minimal background, and its macrostructure should be so familiar to anyone who has tried to teach the academic essay that I hope there will be no undue difficulties in teaching the text.

5. Once again, as in other chapters, students will be sure that they have grasped little to nothing of the text on their first readings and imitations. Don't let them off the hook. First force them to locate where the problems arise (and they will surely be evenly divided between diction and syntax). Read the troubling sentences aloud and force students to explain their meaning. Remind students that this is not esoteric philosophizing; this is a practical court case.

6. As you walk students through the readings, it is crucial that students see the parts of the macrostructure. Ancient rhetoric consistently used the following terms and concepts:

    o *exordium* (opening or introduction)
    o *narratio* (background)
    o *explicatio* (definition of issues)
    o *partitio* (thesis)
    o *~rmatio* (proof or support for the thesis)

○ *refutatio* (refutation)

○ *peroratio* (conclusion)

You might write these on the board. Most of the English versions of these terms will be familiar to the students—ah, they will say, we are talking about essay writing! But it will be important to explain how each part of this structure works on an audience and what its role is in the persuasive argument. It is probably important, too, to emphasize that some of the order can be manipulated—the *refutatio* sometimes comes before the *confirmatio*, for instance. Then it is important that they see how carefully and conscientiously Cicero has built his oration on this form.

With microstructure, it is helpful to explain to the students the interesting features of Latinate syntax—how, in Latin, the words can be presented in almost any order because the endings are what determine the syntactical functions of the words in the sentence. In fact, of course, most Latin sentences have a pretty standard order quite different from English S-V-O order, and most translators attempt to give at least a flavor of that. Students will need help seeing the subordinate clauses at work and imitating how these work.

It might also be interesting for students to note the difference between Latinate and Anglo-Saxon diction, and to attempt to imitate the more Latinate diction here.

Finally, Cicero is of course the master at using all three modes of persuasion: logos, ethos, and pathos. You may use previous chapters to help your students see the workings of these three. In chapter 4 we discovered the ways a writer develops his authority to speak, and so students will by now have a sense of how the ethos of the speaker or writer creates part of his persuasive force. The chapter on scholastic argumentation, chapter 5, was in some ways a primer on the central power of logos. Now, to these two, we are adding in these final two chapters the use of pathos. Have students work through the reading to find places where Cicero favors one or another of these modes, or how he weaves them together skillfully.

The *exordium*. It is always fascinating to students when they see that much of the introductory material here is about Cicero himself and only obliquely (and slyly) sets up the speech about Archias. Cicero foregrounds his own (well-known by this time) expertise in rhetoric, and brings in Archias as one of the sources of his experience with this art.

Yet in the second paragraph he brings in his other subject—poetry—and first comments on it as a surprise subject, since it is seemingly unrelated to rhetoric. Furthermore, Cicero highlights that his speech will deviate from the usual structure of such an oration. Students will find it fascinating that Cicero's audience knew quite well the structure of an oration, expected speakers to follow it, and shaped their listening based on it, so much so that Cicero was careful to alert them in advance of his intended digression.

It is also crucial to point out the many ways that Cicero brings his audience into his oration in the *exordium*. You might wish to discuss the purposes of an introduction and the crucial things an author must do to an audience in the first few words of an essay.

Since the *exordium* is so carefully self-contained in these two paragraphs, it also is a wonderful way to begin work on the microstructures here. Students might be asked to highlight the many logical connectors and cues Cicero gives—"however," "therefore," "a further point, however"— an exercise they should be prepared for after working with the scholastic logical disputation. Or you might ask them to "translate" one of his sentences into Anglo-Saxon diction and "normal" S-V-O word order, then look to see how his voice creates a very different effect.

The *partitio*. It is always a good idea to ask students—perhaps even before working on the exordium—to locate the thesis. Can they find it here, at the end of the second paragraph? Can they understand what he is going to argue, and how this complex syntactical structure sets up his method of proof?

Furthermore, you might ask students to confront this first deviation from normal rhetorical macrostructure. Why insert the thesis here, before the background and definition of issues? What could Cicero expect from his audience that he could do this? Can they see how he has folded the explicatio into the statement of his thesis?

As a side note, students are often interested to find out that *thesis* is actually a Greek term, older even that *partitio*, which was the Latin attempt to translate it. In English we might say "claim" or "point," as in, "Well, what is your point?" or "Here is what I am claiming." I have found that students find a curious comfort in knowing that this term they have struggled with since high school or earlier is actually a word from another language that has a very simple translation.

The *narratio* and *confirmatio*. Once they get this far, students can often look across the white space and immediately see that Cicero begins the *narratio* next—even the term is familiar, and they see that Cicero starts to tell the story of Archias's life in the next four paragraphs. Their comfort level with this reading rises, especially if at this point you show them how to skim the first parts of each paragraph to discover the intention of each.

At the beginning of the fifth paragraph, though, students are brought up short:

ə♥   If the question of his Roman enfranchisement, and the legal position in this respect, are the only issues we have to bear in mind, I
have nothing more to say; and I can close my case.

He can close his case? What happened to the *confirmatio*? Where is
the support, the proof of his thesis? It is a good question to ask the
students here, and it will take some time for them to be able to retreat
to the previous paragraph to see that, in telling the story of Archias's
life, he in fact made his case. The case is proved thus: Archias was
made a citizen of Heraclea; Heraclea had full treaty rights with Rome
so that any citizen of Heraclea was a citizen of Rome; thus Archias is a
Roman citizen. Q.E.D., right? The students will enjoy the subtle, quiet
way Cicero has proved his case, only announcing that it is proven after
he has proven it. Encourage them to construct an imitation that works
in a similar way.

The *refutatio*. By this point in their first read-through and imitation
of the oration, many students had probably lost the thread of Cicero's
point. But by now, patiently working through it, they should be able to
see what Cicero does for the next seven paragraphs, which is to refute
the claims of the prosecution (and the prosecutor, Gratius). It helps to
have students locate, underline, and announce to the class the various
claims that are being refuted. Most are easy to find, as Cicero highlights
them with phrasing such as "You will not surely attempt to deny . . ." and
"Or do you propose to deny that . . ." Others are cued in a more subtle
way. This is a good time to talk about cueing techniques.

The *digression*. Students are next fascinated that almost the entire
remainder of the oration—everything up to the last three paragraphs
of the speech—is a long digression that really does not address the
legal matter before the court at all. This part of the oration is, in fact, an
extended defense of poetry. Of course, like all well-crafted digressions,
it is in fact precisely to the point; Cicero takes on the insular attitudes of
Pompey's followers, the crucial role poetry plays in a republic and culture
(something that is relevant to today's arguments about funding for the
arts), and the role of fame in spurring humans to better deeds. You might
wish to allow students to skip imitating the digression; if they can imitate
the fundamental structures of a classical oration, they are doing very
well indeed, and have proven their skill at college-level writing. But more
advanced classes might be up to the challenge of crafting a digression that
is precisely to the point, so a more careful analysis of this passage in class
might well be in order. I am going to skip it here in the interests of space.

The *peroratio*. Cicero's direct call for judgment announces his turn
to the conclusion, and his summative arguments should be familiar to

students who have had to write conclusions to their essays before. But his direct address to those who will judge the case may seem a fascinating feature for the students to imitate, and the insistent turn again to himself—the "I" rings out strongly at the beginning of each sentence in the last paragraph—provides another strong feature to imitate. Students enjoy working a very close imitation of the final sentence; they sense that this provides the final punctuation to the entire discourse.

7. As I have encouraged in other chapters, do not walk the students through the readings until they have struggled with a draft imitation on their own.

8. Try to avoid having the students read the student imitation before they at least attempt their own. As you read this example, we again refer you to what we noted in the "To The Teacher" section about parody; parody can be a wonderful method of intellectual discovery, and I hope in this late student example to show a student performing it quite well. And in class, when students read a parody, they can often begin to see better than before the structures (both macro and micro) that inform the original.

Notes for chapter 7

1. You could do worse than having a discussion here on these very topics. Students often do not realize that "correctness" in grammar, syntax, usage, etc., does not exist for its own sake, but is important precisely because there is no immediate audience to provide feedback, to ask for further explanation, to question and express misunderstandings. Since an e-mail audience can respond more quickly, there is less need for the formalities of correctness, organization, and so forth; with instant messaging, which approaches the immediacy of spoken conversation, even less. Yet students may know of being caught in a "flame war" when, perhaps inadvertently, they wrote something their audience found offensive or objectionable.

2. This piece of writing is indeed complex, and *after* they have attempted to imitate it, students will still need a great deal of explication of its features. Let us take a look at some of the features students should analyze and attempt to imitate, in the usual fashion.

 ❧ **Macrostructure.** After the salutation (which I discuss below), Gregory begins by seeming to compliment Henry for the latter's devotion to the pope. But look again: he marvels that Henry has sent so many *words* that displayed devotion and humility . . . and yet in action, Gregory says, Henry has shown precisely the opposite. That contrast—between words and deeds, appearance and reality—forms the structure of the first paragraph.

The second paragraph gets its structure from the first words: "it would have been more becoming to you . . ." if Henry had acted properly. Students will have to read carefully to follow the argument. Since Jesus gave power to Peter, and since the pope is Peter's successor, Henry is messing not just with Gregory, but with Peter, the apostle—and eventually, God himself. It's the quoting from the Bible that secures Gregory's authority, but watch the voice he uses, again, to warn Henry.

The third paragraph also uses opposition, opposing the inaccurate view of lay investiture (that it is a burden) with what Gregory calls it: "a truth and light necessary for salvation." It then reminds Henry that he should set a good example.

The fourth paragraph offers an olive branch to Henry; send me a legate who can explain your actions, and all is forgiven (with a hint at the end—again—that Henry could have done this some time ago).

Finally, the fifth paragraph ends with the same opposition, this time between the "hope" that Henry will "improve," and the "warning" of what will happen if he does not. See, Henry? He seems to suggest: you just haven't understood so far; once you understand, you'll see it my way. But don't let the students miss the tough voice backing up that position in the next sentence: "We warn you with a father's love . . ." This was a time before fathers put their sons in "time out" when they were naughty; the warning of a father's love surely suggested that, unless *somebody* started acting right, *somebody* was likely to suffer some unpleasant consequences.

But it is the **microstructure** that truly makes this letter so delicious. Let us explore together some of the features. Again, I cannot be exhaustive here, but these should make a start:

The salutation is crucial in a medieval letter. The medieval *Artes Dictaminis* (guides to letter writing) spent a great deal of time on the salutation, offering different ones for different situations (pope to a bishop; bishop to pope; king to councillor, etc.) because these were moments of high protocol—and crucial rhetorical moments as well. Make sure the students note that the writer's name comes first, and then the addressee, and that appositions allow for interesting descriptions. If the students can grasp at least this, it often jump-starts them into this structure and gets them to pay close attention to the rest of the letter. Here Gregory announces himself as a "bishop," and then the title which his namesake and predecessor, Gregory the Great, invented: *servus servorum Dei*, "servant of the servants of God." It was a title designed to suggest the humility as opposed to the majesty of the papal office, suggesting Christian service as the highest calling. You might have students reflect on why Gregory VII especially calls forth this title now. After his mention of his addressee comes the greeting—but note here that Gregory appends a warning to the greeting, an unusual step that all would have noticed. Notice also how Gregory addresses Henry as "King," but does not add much else to that title. What he does add is a warning: "but with the understanding that he obeys the Apostolic See as becomes a Christian king." (A "see" is a bishopric; as a representative of the apostle Peter, Gregory inhabits an Apostolic See.) So Gregory finishes off the salutation by warning Henry that he ought to obey the pope if he knows what's good for him.

The fundamental feature of the microstructure that all students will need to attempt is the controlled Latinate balanced syntax, the Latinate diction, the official tone thus produced, and the tension it creates between Gregory's real anger and his need to proceed diplomatically. To get them to see the Latinate diction, pick a word and have them give an Anglo-Saxon equivalent: "exceedingly," "legate," "affection."

Students enjoy noting and imitating the royal "we" that Gregory conspicuously uses. You might explore with students the source of this in political ideology—the medieval notion that the king (or here, pope) in some ways "embodies" the entire kingdom, and therefore speaks as the kingdom. The pope, when he speaks as pope, speaks for all the church, so he similarly uses "we."

In the first paragraph, I have noted above the opposition as crucial to the macrostructure. But have students see balance and opposition in each sentence as well. Have them see and imitate how Gregory introduces his list of offenses with "Not to mention other cases."

The second paragraph challenges students to imitate Gregory's quoting of the Bible as proof text. They might consider what texts they would like to quote (or invent and then quote!) in their own imitations. Have them pick apart the argument here, which, boiled down to its essence, is that, when Henry disobeys Gregory, he is disobeying Peter, and eventually, God Himself.

Try to get the students to imitate Gregory's definition of the key term—lay investiture—in their next paragraph, contrasting others' definitions of the term with their own.

In the fourth paragraph, you might encourage the students to see the constant use of the subjunctive, as Gregory outlines what Henry might have done, could have done, would have done, should have done. Have them explore the shift in tone in this paragraph and what causes it.

And in the final paragraph, have the students note the heavy irony: Gregory hopes that Henry will have an "increase of understanding" and benefit from "the long-enduring patience of God"—while hinting that his own patience is wearing thin. Students enjoy the ambiguity when Gregory warns Henry "with a father's love"—what is he suggesting here? What model of fatherhood is he employing? Is there not quite a tension between the "warning" and "love" he holds out? "This is gonna hurt you more than it hurts me," perhaps?

Finally, have the students note and imitate the many triplets in these passages, as in the final sentence.

This hardly exhausts the many features of this complex rhetorical piece. You will surely enjoy finding more things to explore with your students; often it is through their imitations that more features are discovered.

3. Henry's response is just as carefully nuanced as Gregory's letter, even if its tone is more obvious. Students may not see the blatant attack here, or sense in his Latinate phrasing the anger being conveyed, but with some work they begin to see these things quite clearly. Let us work through the piece and see what students might discover and imitate:

The salutation is astonishing in its blunt denunciation of Gregory. Henry declaims his own position immediately—that he has been ordained by God for his kingship. Then he startlingly calls Gregory not by his title, but his given name, Hildebrand, and denies him the papacy entirely. Henry calls him "false monk" because in fact Hildebrand had been a monk; Henry implies that Gregory has been false to his vocation. Monks are supposed to pray, not oppose God's order and thus create confusion.

And in case Gregory missed it—he couldn't have—Henry then goes on to *explain* his rude salutation in the first paragraph! If students can see this, they will have a key to the tone of the entire letter that they will never lose. The Latinate syntax will no longer be seen as simply "formal" and "polite," but rather as an effective vehicle for abuse. They will notice the oppositions in this sentence: "confusion instead of honor, of malediction instead of benediction." A simple change in prefix—"mal" from "bene"—carries the attack here and reinforces the abuse.

In the second paragraph, Henry lists the abuses of Gregory. Students may not see how the paragraph is controlled by "Not only . . . but also." By quoting Gregory the Great back to Gregory VII, he attempts to negate Gregory's placing himself in his predecessor's light.

Here, in the fourth paragraph, Henry paints his own picture of himself by contrast: he is the patient endurer of Gregory's abuses, displaying a humility that Gregory has misunderstood.

The next paragraph builds a crucial step toward the climax of Henry's abuse of Gregory. First, he now states clearly that Gregory has come to a false vocation, opposing his own role as an ordained and anointed king to Hildebrand's false role. He then uses a wonderful *gradatio* to summarize Gregory's faults. Each step leads to another, worse abuse, until, dripping with irony, Henry compares "the throne of peace" (that is, the papal throne) to Gregory's destruction of the peace. Students may at first think that they cannot write an accomplished *gradatio* like this one, but a little brainstorming can help them get started.

Next Henry turns the light on himself, painting his innocence, quoting Saint Peter against the pope, and setting up his central claim: no one but God can judge him unless he deviates from the faith. (Students often enjoy imitating his interjection in this sentence—"may it never happen"—.)

Finally Henry builds to his last series of statements, a set of imperatives ("Descend . . . Relinquish . . . Let another mount . . .") and his rousing call for Gregory's removal as pope. Students may be interested in the fact that Henry calls on Gregory "together with all our bishops."

4. You may or may not decide to have students imitate this third letter; the assignment works well enough with simply one letter and response. I include this partly because students have in the past been interested in how this dispute "all worked out." More on that in a moment. First, students may not immediately realize what they are reading here: it is a letter in which Gregory declares that Henry is no longer ruling with justice and therefore can be legally deposed by his subjects, who are legally released from their vows of loyalty to him. He also excommunicates Henry. Well, no: no pope, or anyone else, ever excommunicates someone from the Catholic Church: what is done is to declare certain views or actions *anathema*, and by holding these views or taking these actions after they have been declared *anathema*, the person excommunicates himself. (The phrase is *anathema sit*, "let him be anathema" who holds these views, crucially a subjunctive construction.) Because of that, this letter is not addressed to Henry; in fact, it ostensibly is addressed to Saint Peter. In it, Gregory defends himself (the first paragraph), releases Henry's subjects and thus makes him deposable (the second paragraph), and then pronounces the excommunication, or *anathema*, in the third. It is in canonical form— that is, the official legal language of the church.

Students may not quite understand the implications of the deposition. Gregory officially releases all of Henry's servants from their oaths of loyalty to Henry; they can now legally prosecute a rebellion. In fact, the document virtually incites them to do so, for it forbids anyone to serve Henry as a king. This was a severe weapon, for it deprived Henry of legal authority in his own lands—somewhat as if the Supreme Court of the United States declared that a president's election were null and void. Henry is now in a dangerous position.

How did this all turn out? Fascinatingly, with that contrast between the grand romantic gesture and the *realpolitik* which so often characterizes the Middle Ages. Henry, aghast at his excommunication—and realizing the perilous situation he was in politically—came across the Alps to where the pope was staying in Northern Italy, at Canossa. There he knelt in the snow, barefoot, outside of the pope's window for three days in the gesture of the penitent begging forgiveness. Finally the pope relented and lifted Henry's excommunication. A romantic ending to the story? Ah, but there is more. For one thing, Henry knew his gesture forced the pope into forgiving him; any priest *must* give absolution to one who confesses and repents (even though there are, and were, serious doubts about whether Henry was truly penitent). So Henry, in kneeing in the snow, had Gregory over the proverbial barrel. And subsequent actions would tend to reinforce this cynical view. Henry regained the loyalty of many princes. The German princes who had set themselves against Henry felt betrayed and elected their own king, Rudolph of Swabia. For three years civil war tore apart Germany, and Gregory declared Rudolph king in 1080, excommunicating Henry again. But this time the excommunication was not taken seriously; Henry was stronger, and he defeated and killed Rudolph. A year later Henry came over the Alps again, this time at the head of an army, and marched upon Rome itself, laying siege to the city for three years, 1081 to 1084. Finally, he crushed the papal forces and Gregory fled to the fortress of Castel Sant'Angelo. His allies, the Normans of South Italy, marched, and Henry's forces retreated, but the Normans, says Tierney, "lived up to their reputation for savage brigandage and looted the whole city, leaving a third of it razed by fire" (55). Pope Gregory died in the south not long after.

About the Author

Gregory L. Roper, an English professor and director of the Writing Program at the University of Dallas, has taught courses in composition, literature, and various genres of writing at the University of Virginia, Ripon College, and Northwest Missouri State University. A medievalist by training, Dr. Roper has published on penitential manuals and their influence on late-medieval literature, including the *Gawain* poet and Chaucer, and has written poetry and prose for such general-interest magazines as *First Things*. His degrees come from the University of Dallas and the University of Virginia.